Today's W... II
Select Readings of Chinese Spotlight News

今日世界面面观
汉语焦点新闻选读

下册

王颖　王志军　徐丽莎　◎编著

北京大学出版社
PEKING UNIVERSITY PRESS

图书在版编目（CIP）数据

今日世界面面观：汉语焦点新闻选读. 下册 / 王颖，王志军，徐丽莎编著. —北京：北京大学出版社，2017.7

ISBN 978-7-301-27973-1

Ⅰ.①今… Ⅱ.①王… ②王… ③徐… Ⅲ.①汉语—阅读教学—对外汉语教学—教材 Ⅳ.①H195.4

中国版本图书馆CIP数据核字（2017）第012948号

书　　　名	今日世界面面观：汉语焦点新闻选读（下册） JINRI SHIJIE MIANMIANGUAN: HANYU JIAODIAN XINWEN XUANDU (XIA CE)
著作责任者	王　颖　王志军　徐丽莎　编著
责 任 编 辑	孙　娴
标 准 书 号	ISBN 978-7-301-27973-1
出 版 发 行	北京大学出版社
地　　　址	北京市海淀区成府路205号　100871
网　　　址	http://www.pup.cn　　新浪微博：@北京大学出版社
电 子 信 箱	zpup@pup.cn
电　　　话	邮购部 62752015　发行部 62750672　编辑部 62753374
印 刷 者	北京大学印刷厂
经 销 者	新华书店 889毫米×1194毫米　16开本　14.5印张　205千字 2017年7月第1版　2017年7月第1次印刷
定　　　价	160.00元（含课本和练习本）

未经许可，不得以任何方式复制或抄袭本书之部分或全部内容。
版权所有，侵权必究
举报电话：010-62752024　电子信箱：fd@pup.pku.edu.cn
图书如有印装质量问题，请与出版部联系，电话：010-62756370

前言

　　本书是为美国大学及其在华中文项目编写的一套新闻时事课教材，同样适用于包括加拿大、英国、澳大利亚、新西兰等在内的其他英语国家。全书共分上下两册，各八个话题，每个话题又分主副两篇课文。一般来说，上册适用于美国大学中文项目的三年级下学期或者四年级上学期，美国外语教学委员会（ACTFL，The American Council on the Teaching of Foreign Languages）设定的"中级–高"（Intermediate-high）到"高级–低"（Advanced-low）水平的学习者；下册适用于美国大学中文项目的四年级上学期或者下学期，美国外语教学委员会设定的"高级–中"（Advanced-mid）到"高级–高"（Advanced-high）水平的学习者。

　　以报刊新闻作为高级汉语的教材具有诸多优点：语料真实、时效性强、实用性强、结合现实生活紧密、话题性强、便于学以致用等。但是受新闻本身求"新"求"快"特点的制约，不论是报纸上还是网络上登出的新闻原始材料大多是"急就章"，文字疏于仔细推敲和反复锤炼。另外，极强的"即时性"也使得不少新闻刚成为热点又迅速地"冷却"下来，昨日的新闻旋即成为今日的"旧闻"，不再引起读者的关注。本套教材本着"与时俱进""细选精编"的原则，力图发挥新闻材料的优势，同时克服和弥补其弱点。具体说来，这套教材具备以下一些特点：

　　在话题方面，选材虽来源于各大新闻网络，但文字都经过我们反复增删、加工和修改。教材的主要内容都是既体现了新闻的时效性又受到了大众持续关注的热门话题；既关注到中国和美国的焦点话题，又做到一个话题多个视角，突显问题的多元性和文化交叉的层面；既提供精读课文，又选有泛读或者扩展阅读材料。比如，环境污染问题是一个受到持续关注的话题，在这个话题下，我们选编的主副课文分别聚焦于近期在北京的雾霾和太平洋出现的白色污染——"塑料岛"上，而反映北京雾霾的主课文还讨论、比较了英国雾都伦敦的空气污染问题和历史。又如，枪支政策是美国长久以来一直"吸引眼球"的热点。在这个话题下，我们选编的主课文报道、评论了近年来美国校园频发的枪击案件，而副课文则重点讨论了美国民众对控枪政策的不同态度。由于同时关注中美两国时事，"时效性"和"持续性"兼顾，主副课文并存，做到了内容丰富、视角多广、观点深刻，便于在课上深入讨论和在课下延展学习。

在语言方面，教材将选词标准设定在汉语水平测试丙级以上，词频800以上。每课的主课文后都带有词汇和句法注释，旨在帮助老师教授和学生了解新闻阅读的难点和重点。词汇讲解从最小的语素单位开始，逐步过渡到书面语和口语表达，成语、四字格和虚词的使用等。句法分析则侧重在新闻书面语的长句上。

另外值得一提的是，教材的课文和生词都配有录音，便于学生掌握正确的发音、声调、轻重音，以及适当的停顿。为方便老师和学生使用，教材中所有的课后习题均单独成册。我们甚至考虑到了教材数字化的可能性，比方说，练习本中的习题大部分可以放到校园课件网上采用机改的方式。使用这套教材的老师也可以在麻省五校联盟的网上（https://commons.mtholyoke.edu/video/）找到一些我们选编的有关新闻话题的视频。我们计划继续增加和完善这方面的资料，提供给选择我们这套教材的师生使用。

王颖　王志军　徐丽莎
于美国麻省先锋谷

PREFACE

This is a set of books designed for a newspaper reading class offered by Chinese programs in the United States and American study-abroad language programs within China. They can also be used by learners in other English-speaking countries such as Canada, United Kingdom, Australia, and New Zealand. The whole set includes two volumes; each volume contains eight topics, and each topic has a main text and a supplementary text. Generally speaking, the target users of this set of books are students who have completed two and half years of Chinese (or those who have completed the first semester of third-year Chinese) in a regular Chinese program from an American or any other English-speaking university. Volume 1 of this set of books is designed for intermediate-high to advanced-low learners according to ACTFL (The American Council on the Teaching of Foreign Languages); Volume 2 is designed for advanced-mid to advanced-high learners.

Using newspapers as instructional materials for advanced Chinese learning has several recognizable merits, including the authenticity, up-to-datedness, topicality, and practicality of newspaper language and information as well as its close connection and applicability to everyday life. However, because of the "newness" and swift turnaround that characterize newswriting, original publications in printed newspapers or online sources are all compositions created in a short timeframe and therefore lack careful deliberation and refinement. This time constraint and need for immediacy can quickly render hot topics cool; yesterday's breaking news becomes today's old news and no longer attracts readers' attention. Based on the principles of "keeping pace with the times" and "careful selection and editing," this set of books aims to make full use of the merits of newspaper materials while remedying their defects. Specifically, the content and form of the books demonstrate the following features.

The materials for these books have been selected from various major newspapers and online sources, but have been repeatedly and meticulously mended, revised, and refined by the editors. In material selection and content, this set of books not only reflects the transient nature of news reports, but also grasps long-lasting "hot topics"; it not only focuses on pressing issues for both China and the United States, but also brings forth diverse perspectives and cross-cultural aspects of these issues. Additionally, it not only provides careful and thorough reading of texts, but also includes extensive reading materials for each selected topic. For example, environmental pollution has been a long-time news topic. For this topic, we selected a main text that focuses on the air pollution in Beijing in recent years and a supplementary text that deals with "white pollution" in the Pacific—specifically, the ocean's "plastic island." Furthermore, within the main text, we compared Beijing's current air pollution with London's similar pollution problems in the past. Another issue that has continuously attracted readers' attention is the policy of owning private guns in the United States. For this topic, we reflected in the main text on the recent and frequent gun shootings that have happened on American campuses while discussing in the supplementary text the different attitudes Americans have toward gun control. Because of the dual focus on China and the United States, the consideration given to both the transiency and continuity of news issues, and the inclusion of both main and supplementary texts, this set of textbooks is rich in content, inclusive in perspective, and thought-provoking in its views. It is highly useful for deep and extensive discussion and study both inside and outside the classroom.

The vocabulary of this set of textbooks is set at the third level of the HSK (Chinese Proficiency Test) with a word frequency of 800 and above. To help instructors and students understand difficult and important points of vocabulary and grammar, vocabulary and sentence-pattern explanations are provided for each main text. The vocabulary section includes an explanation of morphemes, written and oral expressions, idioms, four-character phrases, and function words, while the sentence pattern section analyzes the long sentence structure of written news reports.

What is also worth mentioning is that the texts and vocabulary lists are accompanied by audio-recordings to assist with pronunciation, tones, stress, and pauses. For the convenience of our users, each volume provides a workbook. We have even considered the possibilities of digital adaptation of these materials and the incorporation of online resources. For example, a large portion of the vocabulary and grammar exercises can be adapted to an online format using learning management systems on campus. Users of this set of books can also find several related news videos on the website of the Massachusetts Five College Consortium (https://commons.mtholyoke.edu/video). We plan to continue to increase and enhance the online materials and provide them to our users freely.

Ying Wang, Zhijun Wang, Lisha Xu
October, 2015 at Pioneer Valley, Massachusetts, USA

缩略表 *Abbreviations for Parts of Speech*

abbr.	abbreviation	num.	numeral
adj.	adjective	on.	onomatopoeia
ad.p.	adverbial phrase	part.	particle
adv.	adverbs	pr.	pronoun
adj.p.	adjective phrase	pref.	prefix
attr.	attributive phrase	prep.	preposition
aux.	auxiliary word	r.f.	reduplicated form
b.f.	bound form	suf.	suffix
conj.	conjunction	v.	verb
f.e.	fixed expression	v(c)	verb-complement compound
intj.	interjection	v.o.	verb-object compound
m(n)	measure word for noun	v./n.	dynamic of multi-category words
m(v)	measure word for verb		(verb & noun)
n.	noun	v.p.	verb phrase
n.p.	noun phrase		

目录

第 1 课　　　经济改革如何与危机赛跑　/1

主课文

/1　　经济改革如何与危机赛跑

词语注释

/6　　⊙ 语素：下-，-势/势-，外-，-点，-机/机-

/7　　⊙ 虚词及句型：自（从）……以来，不仅……而且……，所，以……为……，并，由，于（1、2），既……也/又……

副课文

/12　　沃尔玛在中国

第 2 课　　　浅析中国同性恋现象　/17

主课文

/17　　浅析中国同性恋现象

词语注释

/24　　⊙ 语素：-恋，跨-，非-，-感，-意识，-心

/25　　⊙ 四字格和成语：大逆不道，不屑一顾

/26　　⊙ 虚词及句型：既然……就……，同……有关，被……所……，对于

副课文

/28　　同性恋在美国

I

第3课　3D打印与未来生活　/34

主课文

/34　3D打印与未来生活

词语注释

/40　⊙ **语素：** -家，-卡，复-，-具，-品，-域

/41　⊙ **四字格和成语：** 无所不能，高高在上，遥不可及，疼痛不已

/43　⊙ **虚词及句型：** 该，当中，小到……大到……，……之一

副课文

/45　情感慢递店　浪漫寄心情

第4课　在线大学：在网络时代实现"有教无类"的梦想　/49

主课文

/49　在线大学：在网络时代实现"有教无类"的梦想

词语注释

/56　⊙ **语素：** 免-，-型，-者，首-，-级，增-，入-，-书，重-，-费，互-

/58　⊙ **四字格和成语：** 有教无类，千千万万，随时随地，与此同时，侃侃而谈，兴趣盎然，刮目相看

/61　⊙ **虚词及句型：** 在于，不论，于（3），于是，之所以……，为（1）

副课文

/64　扎克伯格清华秀中文

第5课　奥运会与兴奋剂 /69

主课文
/69　奥运会与兴奋剂

词语注释
/75　⊙ 语素：-剂，-器，-物，-牌，-坛，-手
/76　⊙ 四字格和成语：源远流长，精疲力竭，坚持不懈，斗智斗勇
/77　⊙ 虚词及句型：为（2），因……而……，随之，以，只要……就……

副课文
/80　现代人和慢运动

第6课　道德还是自由：美国堕胎合法化之争 /85

主课文
/85　道德还是自由：美国堕胎合法化之争

词语注释
/91　⊙ 语素：-期，-人，反-，-形，-药
/92　⊙ 四字格和成语：愈演愈烈，背道而驰
/93　⊙ 虚词及句型：无异于，而，否则，被视为，对……而言，为（3、4）

副课文
/96　女青年意外怀孕引起社会关注

第7课　美国金牌主播因"说谎门"而"下课" /101

主课文

/101　美国金牌主播因"说谎门"而"下课"

词语注释

/107　⊙ **语素**：-薪，-界，-弹，-机，亲-，失-，受-，-门

/109　⊙ **四字格和成语**：九死一生，如日中天，涂脂抹粉，至高无上

/111　⊙ **虚词及句型**：如此，以便，尤其

副课文

/113　三人行，必有一自媒体

第8课　外媒热议：中国开放"二胎"政策 /118

主课文

/118　外媒热议：中国开放"二胎"政策

词语注释

/124　⊙ **语素**：-研/研-，-媒/媒-，-价/价-，-减/减-，-养/养-

/125　⊙ **四字格和成语**：~~不一，大同小异，相提并论，一成不变，显而易见，水涨船高

/128　⊙ **虚词及句型**：一直，一旦，导致，一向

副课文

/130　云南"光棍村"：人口性别比例失衡一案

/135　**生词索引**

/165　**专有名词索引**

经济改革如何与危机赛跑

第1课

主课文 Main Text

2008年爆发的经济危机是自上个世纪三十年代经济大萧条以来最严重的一次，对全球经济产生了巨大的影响，被人们称为"金融海啸"。中国政府在危机爆发后实施了一系列经济政策，成功应对了这场危机，并为世界经济的恢复和发展作出了贡献。数据表明，中国不仅遏制了经济的下滑趋势，而且在2009年上半年让国内生产总值增速达到7.1%。但同时，数据也显示中国经济发展还存在不稳定和不平衡的态势。在经济危机的威胁下，如何保持经济的稳定和可持续发展，是当今中国所面临的一个重大挑战。

中国经济在改革开放以后高速发展，甚至被外媒称为"中国模式"。这种经济模式以市场为经济活动主体，国家对市场进行监督，扮演"领导"的角色，确定任务和目标，并引导经济向着实现这些目标的方向前进。其最重要的特点是对外贸易和投资开放，以及融入国际经济的开放模式。另外，中国面对各种形势的灵活性与适应能力，也是中国经济成功的关键之一。但是，当前中国经济发展中的三个重要因素，出口、投资和消费都遇到了一些问题。出口遇到的问题一方面是由人民币升值造成的成本优势下降。现在中国不少出口企业都纷纷到越南等地去开工厂了，其目的就是要降低成本。另一方面就是国际贸易不平衡，大量出口引起其他国家的贸易保护主义抬头和贸易壁垒设置。投资遇到的问题主要是中国的钢铁、水泥、煤炭等行业的产能过剩。研究显示，31个行业中的28个都产能过剩。所以想单纯依靠投资拉动经济发展是比较困难的。在中国，消费只占国民生产总值的三分之一。老百姓看病、上学等大额消费支出都需要由自己支付，所以老百姓就得攒着钱。这是消费力低的根本原因。

　　面对这些问题，应该采取哪些改革措施呢？首先，政府应该调整经济结构，扩大内需，而不是将出口作为提高国民生产总值的主要经济方式。同时为人们提供教育和医疗保障，以提高消费力。其次，允许民营企业进入各种行业，并提高其法律地位，来提升其市场竞争力。与此同时，在城镇化的进程中为农民提供更多的保障。再次，政府应该保障一个公开、透明的市场，为经济发展提供一个良好的环境。除此之外，还有一个重要的举措就是要发展"绿色经济"。在探求经济复苏之路上，"绿色经济""低碳经济"已经成为很多国家的关键词。美国将致力于把新能源、低碳经济作为未来经济的增长点。欧盟也把推动科技创新作为提升竞争力的关键。日本则提出了"引领世界二氧化碳低排放革命"的口号。日本政府高达56.8万亿日元的经济刺激计划中，有6万亿日元用于绿色能源产业的发展。由此看来，发展"绿色经济"既是着眼于未来的考虑，也是中国经济在未来保持稳步发展的一个重要改革措施。

　　纵观历史，每次大的经济危机都曾重创世界经济，同时又催生新的发展机遇。所以，只有把握机遇并实行有效的经济改革才能在与危机的赛跑中取胜。

Lesson 1 第1课 经济改革如何与危机赛跑

讨论题 Discussion

根据课文内容回答下列问题
(Please answer the following questions based on the text)

1. 2008年爆发的世界经济危机对中国的经济发展有什么样的影响？
2. 在改革开放以后，中国的经济发展被外媒称为"中国模式"。这种模式有什么特点？
3. 中国经济发展中的三个重要因素是什么？目前这三个方面遇到了哪些问题？
4. 在作者看来，面临经济发展中的问题，中国政府应该采取哪些改革措施？
5. 在美国看来，未来经济的增长点是什么？美国、欧盟和日本在这个方面是怎么做的？
6. 作者认为应该怎么做才能在与经济危机的赛跑中取胜？

生词 New Words

1	赛跑	賽跑	sàipǎo	v.	to race
2	爆发	爆發	bàofā	v.	to erupt, to break out
3	萧条	蕭條	xiāotiáo	adj.	(economic) in depression
4	全球		quánqiú	n.	whole world
5	海啸	海嘯	hǎixiào	n.	tsunami, tidal wave
6	系列		xìliè	n.	series, set
7	作出		zuòchū	v(c)	to make, to work out, to make with

8	遏制		èzhì	v.	to restrain, to control
9	下滑		xiàhuá	v.	to slide, to decline
10	趋势	趨勢	qūshì	n.	trend, current, tendency
11	上半年		shàngbànnián	n.	first half of a year
12	总值	總值	zǒngzhí	n.	gross or total value
13	增速		zēngsù	n.	growth rate
14	平衡		pínghéng	n./v.	balance, equilibrium; to counterpoise
15	态势	態勢	tàishì	n.	state, stance, posture
16	可持续	可持續	kěchíxù	adj.	sustainable
17	高速		gāosù	attr.	high speed, super-speed
18	媒		méi	b.f.	media
19	模式		móshì	n.	model, pattern, mode
20	主体	主體	zhǔtǐ	n.	centerpiece, main body
21	对外	對外	duì wài	v.o.	external, foreign
22	融入		róngrù	v.	to merge into, to integrate into
23	升值	昇值	shēngzhí	v.	to rise in value
24	优势	優勢	yōushì	n.	superiority, advantage
25	贸易保护主义	貿易保護主義	màoyì bǎohù zhǔyì	n.p.	trade protectionism
26	抬头	抬頭	tái tóu	v.o.	to gain ground, to rise
27	壁垒	壁壘	bìlěi	n.	barrier
28	设置	設置	shèzhì	v./n.	to set up, to install; sets, settings
29	钢铁	鋼鐵	gāngtiě	n.	iron and steel
30	产能	產能	chǎnnéng	n.	capacity of production

31	过剩	過剩	guòshèng	v.	excess, overabundance, surplus
32	单纯	單純	dānchún	adj.	simple
33	拉动	拉動	lādòng	v.	to pull, to drive, to promote
34	国民	國民	guómín	n.	people of a nation
35	支出		zhīchū	v./n.	to expend; expenses, disbursement
36	攒	攢	zǎn	v.	to accumulate, to save
37	内需	內需	nèixū	n.	domestic market demand
38	医疗	醫療	yīliáo	v.	to take medical treatment
39	民营	民營	mínyíng	attr.	privately run (of enterprises), nongovernmental business
40	提升	提昇	tíshēng	v.	to promote, to upgrade, to elevate
41	城镇	城鎮	chéngzhèn	n.	cities and towns
42	进程	進程	jìnchéng	n.	course, process, progress
43	透明		tòumíng	adj.	transparent
44	举措	舉措	jǔcuò	n.	move, act, initiative
45	探求		tànqiú	v.	to pursue, to search for, to seek
46	复苏	復蘇	fùsū	v.	to resuscitate
47	致力		zhì lì	v.o.	to work for, to devote one's efforts to
48	引领	引領	yǐnlǐng	v.	to lead
49	二氧化碳		èryǎnghuàtàn	n.	carbon dioxide
50	刺激		cìjī	n./v.	stimulation, stimulus; to provoke, to excite
51	着眼	著眼	zhuóyǎn	v.	to have one's eyes on (a goal), to focus on
52	稳步	穩步	wěnbù	adv.	with steady steps, steadily

53	纵观	縱觀	zòngguān	v.	to make a comprehensive survey, to take an overall view
54	重创	重創	zhòngchuāng	v.	to inflict heavy losses on
55	催生		cuīshēng	v.	to expedite delivery
56	机遇	機遇	jīyù	n.	opportunity
57	把握		bǎwò	v./n.	to grasp, to seize; certainty of success
58	取胜	取勝	qǔshèng	v.	to win, to succeed

专有名词 Proper nouns

| 1 | 越南 | | Yuènán | Vietnam |
| 2 | 欧盟 | 歐盟 | Ōuméng | European Union |

词语注释 Vocabulary and Grammar explanations

语素 (morphemes)

下-：下降。(to descend)

> 例 下滑　下跌　下落　下沉

-势/势-：1. 势力。(power; influence)

> 例 权势　优势　劣势　弱势　强势　趋炎附势　势族

　　2. 态势。(tendency)

> 例 形势　趋势　走势　势头

外-：外边的，外国。(outer; foreign)

> 例 外媒　外企　外国　外宾　外商　外地　外星　外人　外套

-点：1.一定的处所或程度的标点。(point)

> 例 据点　沸点　增长点　聚会点　报考点

2.零售店。(store)

> 例 销售点　批发点　零售点　代售点　营业网点

3.方面。(aspect)

> 例 重点　特点　热点

-机/机-：机会。(chance; opportunity)

> 例 危机　时机　良机　机遇　机会　机缘

虚词及句型 (function words and sentence patterns)

• 自（从）……以来　since...

介词性词组，表示从过去某时直到现在，或特指某一段时期。常见的形式是：自（从）+时间/事件+以来。

This is a prepositional phrase that indicates "from a specific past time to now" or points to a specific time period. The often seen form is: "自（从）+ time/event + 以来".

(1) 2008年爆发的经济危机是自上个世纪三十年代经济大萧条以来最严重的一次，对全球经济产生了巨大的影响，被人们称为"金融海啸"。

(2) 自大学毕业以来，她一直在一家国际银行工作。

(3) 自2013年以来，中国政府开始调整生育政策。

(4) 自改革开放以来，中国的经济有了快速的发展。

● **不仅……而且……**　not only…but also…

固定用法。用法同"不但……而且……"，表示递进关系，连接两个小句或者形容词等，多用于书面语。

This is a fixed expression whose usage is the same as "不但……而且……". This expression indicates a progressive relationship and connects two short sentences or adjectives, etc. It is usually used in written expression.

 (1) 数据表明，中国不仅遏制了经济的下滑趋势，而且在2009年上半年让国内生产总值增速达到7.1%。

(2) 央企存在着薪酬结构不合理、监管体制不够健全等问题。如果这些问题不能得到解决，不仅会影响企业的改革发展，而且会影响社会的公平正义。

(3) 据报道，观看伦敦2014跨年烟火的人数达到了50万人，这不仅令人不安，而且存在着潜在危险。

(4) 谷歌Android One计划不仅无法进入中国，而且在东南亚等其他地区的发展前景也很渺茫。

(5) 她不仅聪慧，而且善良。

- **所**　that, which, where, who, what

  助词，用于书面语。用在及物动词前，使"所+动词"成为名词性短语。

  This is a particle used in written expression and placed before transitive verbs, making "所 + verb" a noun phrase.

  > (1) 在经济危机的威胁下，如何保持经济的稳定和可持续发展，是当今中国所面临的一个重大挑战。
  > (2) Windows系统的平板电脑已经越来越被大家所接受，很多厂商都开始生产Windows平板电脑。
  > (3) 我们开会时会讨论你所提出的问题。
  > (4) 环境污染所带来的危害是非常严重的。

- **以……为……**　to count as; to consider as; to treat as

  固定用法。连接名词和名词性短语，等于"把……作为……"或"认为……是……"。

  This is a fixed expression that is used to connect nouns or noun phrases. It means "to count…as", "to consider…as", "to treat…as", or "to regard…as". It is equivalent to "把……作为……" or "认为……是……".

  > (1) 这种经济模式以市场为经济活动主体，国家对市场进行监督，扮演"领导"的角色。
  > (2) 这名男子以无钱看病为由进行诈骗。
  > (3) 她决定结婚后以家庭生活为中心，而事业是第二位的。
  > (4) 在二战中，很多知识分子以笔墨为武器，写文章谴责侵略者的罪行。

● 并 and

连词，表示更进一层的意思。多用于连接并列的双音节动词。连接小句时，小句的主语承前省略（见例1和例2）。

This is a conjunction; it indicates progressive relation and is used between two disyllabic verbs. When it is used to connect short sentences (clauses), the subject should be brought forward (see examples 1 and 2).

> (1) 这种经济模式以市场为经济活动主体，国家对市场进行监督，扮演"领导"的角色，确定任务和目标，并引导经济向着实现这些目标的方向前进。
>
> (2) 对于在事故中受伤的学生，学校均已安排专人陪护，并将对学生进行心理辅导。
>
> (3) 会议讨论并通过了今年的工作计划。
>
> (4) 据新华社报道，一名日本女学者在印度调研期间遭多名男子轮奸并被囚禁近3个星期，2014年年底才逃脱报案。

● 由 by; through

介词，多用于书面语。1) 引进施动者，跟名词结合（见例1、例2）；2) 表示方式、原因和来源，跟名词结合（见例3、例4）；3) 表示处所起点或来源，跟处所词语结合（见例5、例6）。

This is a preposition used in written expression. 1) It introduces the agent and is followed by a noun (see examples 1 and 2); 2) It indicates manner, reason, and source, and is followed by a noun (see examples 3 and 4); 3) It indicates a starting point or source and is followed by a location word (see examples 5 and 6).

> (1) 老百姓看病、上学等大额消费支出都需要由自己支付，所以老百姓就得攒着钱。

(2) 这个问题由大家讨论解决。
(3) 这次的飞机事故不知是由什么原因造成的。
(4) 小明对二战的历史特别有兴趣，这科的成绩最好。他的父母由这件事得到启发，决定鼓励他学历史专业。
(5) 飞机明天早上七点由首都机场起飞。
(6) 这艘货轮由上海起航，目的地是东北大连。

● 于（1、2）

介词，用于书面表达。1）表示方向，目标。常见的形式是"于+名词、动词、形容词短语"（见例1至例4）；2）表示对象：对，向，常跟名词、代词、动词短语组合（见例5至例8）。

This is a preposition and is usually used in written expression. 1) It indicates direction or objective; the often seen forms include: "于 + noun/verb/adjective phrase" (see examples 1 to 4). 2) It is used as "towards"; the often seen form is: "于 + noun/pronoun/verb phrase" (see examples 5 to 8).

例 致力于 用于 献身于 从事于 着眼于 有助于 有利于 不利于 有愧于 有求于 习惯于

例 (1) 美国将致力于把新能源、低碳经济作为未来经济的增长点。
(2) 日本政府高达56.8万亿日元的经济刺激计划中，有6万亿日元用于绿色能源产业的发展。
(3) 他对自己要求不高，习惯于满足。
(4) 如果没有发生战争，他会一辈子都从事于科学研究工作。
(5) 发展"绿色经济"既是着眼于未来的考虑，也是中国经济在未来保持稳步发展的一个重要改革措施。

(6) 咱们能不能面谈？我不大习惯于写邮件。

(7) 他有求于我，所以对我毕恭毕敬的。

(8) 我们不能满足于现状。

- 既……也/又…… not only...but also...

固定用法。后一部分表示进一步补充说明，连接两个结构相同或相似的词语和小句，前后主语一致。

This is a fixed expression. Its second part is a supplementary and explanation to the first part. The structure connects two words or clauses (short sentences) with the same structure, sharing the same subject.

(1) 发展"绿色经济"既是着眼于未来的考虑，也是中国经济在未来保持稳步发展的一个重要改革措施。

(2) 在尼泊尔东南部冻死的九人中，既有七八十岁的老人，也有四五十岁的中年人，甚至儿童。

(3) 让孩子多交朋友，既能培养孩子的人际交往能力，又能培养孩子分享的精神。

(4) 这位老师既严格又耐心，学生们都很喜欢她。

副课文 Supplementary Text

沃尔玛在中国

沃尔玛1962年成立，是全世界最大的连锁零售公司。它自1996年进入中国以来，就大力开设连锁店。据统计，沃尔玛在中国经营了约400家分店。2012年，它的销售额约达100亿美元。

沃尔玛的成功有多方面的因素。其中最重要的就是"天天平价"的销售理念。沃尔玛是怎样实现其"天天平价"承诺的呢？它不是处理积压商品或销售质量差的商品，而是通过不断降低成本来实现的。具体来说，首先，实现采购本地化。在中国，沃尔玛商店销售的95%的商品都是"中国造"，这样，既节约成本，又适应当地顾客的消费习惯。其次，建立现代化的物流配送中心。运用高科技，实现电脑化统一管理，从而大幅提高效率，降低成本。最后，降低营业成本。无论在沃尔玛的办公室里，还是在连锁店里，都没有豪华的装修。为了保持低价位，沃尔玛将损耗降到最低限度。这些策略使得沃尔玛的经营成本大大低于其他同行业竞争者。除此之外，在中国，沃尔玛还积极开展社区服务和慈善公益活动，向各种慈善公益事业捐献了超过7700万元的物品和资金。沃尔玛在中国的经营始终坚持本地采购，提供更多的就业机会，支持当地制造业，促进当地经济的发展。

最近，该公司宣布将于2014年至2016年间，在中国开设110家分店。据英国《金融时报》报道，除了开设分店以外，沃尔玛旗下山姆会员店也将其目标瞄准了中国市场。在中国，由于交通堵塞和市区停车难等问题，消费者更倾向于开车去郊区购物。在大城市郊区的山姆会员店就为消费者提供了方便。另外，沃尔玛已计划对其当前的运营模式进行调整，变得更加创新，从而适应消费者市场的快速变化。其中包括：削减成本，以建立起更强大的企业；更加注重提高新鲜食品和各类杂货的质量，建立一流的食品安全方案。到2014年10月份之前，中国所有的沃尔玛超市都可以使用配有质量监控和合格监管的水果与干果配送中心。作为扩张计划的一部分，沃尔玛承诺通过新增门店和配送中心为中国创造1.9万个工作岗位。沃尔玛中国区副总裁雷布·雷西表示："我们希望在中国获得更好的收益。"

讨论题 Discussion

根据课文内容回答下列问题
(Please answer the following questions based on the text)

1. 沃尔玛是一家什么样的公司？
2. 沃尔玛成功最重要原因是什么？
3. 沃尔玛是怎么做到销售平价商品的？
4. 沃尔玛为中国的慈善公益事业做了什么？
5. 沃尔玛旗下山姆会员店有什么经营计划？
6. 根据沃尔玛未来在中国的计划，并根据网上的相关资料，分析一下沃尔玛在中国的前景。

生词 New Words

1	连锁	連鎖	liánsuǒ	adj./attr.	chain, interlocked elements, linkage
2	零售		língshòu	v.	to retail, to sell retail
3	开设	開設	kāishè	v.	to open (shop)
4	平价	平價	píngjià	n.	parity, fair (state) price
5	承诺	承諾	chéngnuò	v./n.	to agree to do sth.; promise, pledge
6	积压	積壓	jīyā	v.	to keep long in stock, to overstock
7	本地		běndì	n.	local
8	物流		wùliú	n.	logistics
9	配送		pèisòng	v.	to take a delivery

14

Lesson 1

经济改革如何与危机赛跑

	简体	繁體	Pinyin	词性	English
10	豪华	豪華	háohuá	adj.	luxurious
11	装修	裝修	zhuāngxiū	v./n.	to decorate; decoration
12	价位	價位	jiàwèi	n.	price level
13	损耗	損耗	sǔnhào	v./n.	to cause loss; wear and tear
14	限度		xiàndù	n.	limitation, limit
15	策略		cèlüè	n.	tactics, strategy
16	公益		gōngyì	n	public welfare
17	捐献	捐獻	juānxiàn	v.	to contribute, to donate
18	物品		wùpǐn	n.	article, goods
19	旗下		qíxià	n.	subordinate, those under one's command
20	瞄准	瞄準	miáozhǔn	v(c)	to aim at
21	堵塞		dǔsè	v.	to stop up, to jam, to block up
22	市区	市區	shìqū	n.	urban district, downtown
23	购物	購物	gòu wù	v.o.	to go shopping
24	运营	運營	yùnyíng	v.	to be in operation, to operate (or run) in an organized way
25	削减	削減	xuējiǎn	v.	to cut down, to reduce
26	杂货	雜貨	záhuò	n.	sundry goods, groceries
27	一流		yīliú	attr.	first-rate, top-notch
28	超市		chāoshì	n.	supermarket
29	配		pèi	v./b.f.	to allot; to provide with
30	监控	監控	jiānkòng	v.	to supervise and control
31	合格		hégé	adj.	qualified, up to standard
32	监管	監管	jiānguǎn	v./n.	to supervise, to keep watch on; supervision

33	干果	乾果	gānguǒ	n.	dried fruits
34	扩张	擴張	kuòzhāng	v.	to expand, to extend, to enlarge
35	增		zēng	v./b.f.	to increase, to add
36	门店	門店	méndiàn	n.	store
37	总裁	總裁	zǒngcái	n.	president (of a company)
38	收益		shōuyì	n.	income, profit, earnings, gains

专有名词 Proper nouns

1	沃尔玛	沃爾瑪	Wò'ěrmǎ	Walmart
2	金融时报	金融時報	Jīnróng Shíbào	*Financial Times*
3	山姆会员店	山姆會員店	Shānmǔ Huìyuán Diàn	Sam's Club
4	雷布·雷西		Léibù Léixī	Ray Bracy

浅析中国同性恋现象

第 2 课

主课文 Main Text

2008年5月15日上午，美国加利福尼亚州最高法院裁定同性婚姻合法。基于这一裁决，加州成为全美第二个法律认可同性婚姻的州。当地时间6月17日，加州知名华裔女作家谢汉兰与伴侣在旧金山市政厅司法官的主持下举行了结婚仪式。

爱白网在第一时间报道了这则消息。爱白网是为同性恋、双性恋及跨性别群体提供资讯的中文网站。不少人在留言里发出了"好羡慕""好感动"的感慨。在中国，尽管同性恋依然是一个非主流的禁忌话题，但是中国社会对同性恋的宽容度正在逐步扩大。

同性恋者的压力

据权威估计，中国有二千七百万左右的同性恋。由于主流社会的偏见与歧视，绝大多数的同性恋者不得不隐匿自己的身份，仍然戴着面具生活。他们的压力主要来自以下几个方面：

首先，中国传统伦理道德认为，"男大当婚，女大当嫁"①"不孝有三，无后为大"②。由于同性恋无法生育子女，因而属于"大逆不道"的范畴。这使得很多同性恋者认为目前最大的压力不是来自于社会，而是来自于家庭，因为大多数父母都难以接受这个现实。其次，中国社会强调羞耻感和群体意识，如果同性恋的身份暴露，同性恋者的亲友会为此感到没面子。最后，由于在宣传上常把艾滋病与同性恋相联系，加深了一些缺乏相关知识的人们对同性恋的歧视。

异性恋者的宽容

但总的来说，和西方相比，中国从古至今对同性恋都采取了相对宽容的态度。在中国的几千年历史中，从来没有残酷迫害同性恋的记录，从未有人因同性恋被判为死刑，公众舆论对同性恋一向比较温和。中国公众对同性恋的接纳程度比较高，历史和文化方面的原因大致有以下几点：

首先，中国历史上曾有不少对同性恋的记载。春秋战国时社会有崇尚美男之风，还形成了成语典故。如"余桃"③"断袖"④等成为同性恋的代名

---

① "男大当婚，女大当嫁"，or in English, "upon growing up, every male should take a wife and every female should take a husband", is a common saying in China.

② "不孝有三，无后为大"，or in English, "there are three forms of unfilial conduct, of which the worst is to have no descendants", is a quotation from the first part of "Lilou" in *Mencius*（孟子·离娄上）.

③ 余桃 yútáo or "the leftover peach", recorded in *Hanfeizi*, refers to Mi Zixia (弥子瑕)，a beautiful youth cherished by Duke Ling of Wei（卫灵公 540–493 B.C.）. Mi Zixia once shared an already bitten but delicious peach with the duke, who appreciated the gesture. However, once the mature Mi Zixia lost his beauty, the duke looked back on this event and regarded Mi as insincere.

④ 断袖 duànxiù or "cutting off the sleeve" refers to Emperor Ai of the Han Dynasty（汉哀帝 25–1 B.C.）who adored a catamite named Dong Xian (董贤). One morning, the emperor got up early to go hunting, but his sleeve was trapped under Dong Xian，who was still soundly sleeping in the same bed. The emperor cut off his sleeve in order not to wake him.

词。其次，中国人没有普遍信仰的宗教。大部分中国人往往以平常心和直觉来评价人与事，认为同性恋既然不会伤害他人，就与他人无关。第三，这种态度也许同中国人的民族性格有关。中国文化源远流长，中国人对自己的主流文化很有信心，从不担心被非主流文化所影响。人们对于非主流文化往往采取不屑一顾的态度，而不至于残酷迫害它。第四，中国同性恋的法律地位模糊不清。对于同性恋，中国没有明确的法律条文加以禁止。

中国官方一份最新调查显示，中国民众对同性恋的接受度达九成，超过美国的86%。2005年9月7日，复旦大学在全国高校中率先开设了同性恋研究的选修课；2005年，作为中国政府主流媒体代表的中央电视台播出了与同性恋有关的节目《以生命的名义》；2006年，中央电视台音乐频道播出了以同性恋为题材的音乐电视《爱不分》；2007年，凤凰卫视的访谈性栏目《鲁豫有约》以《同志爱人》《拉拉的故事》以及《亲密爱人》等为题制作了几期以同性恋者为被访者的节目。与此同时，越来越多的同志网站、酒吧和求助热线不断产生，像《点》《Les+》《同语》等同性恋读物也陆续出版。目前，越来越多同性恋题材的华语电影被搬上了大银幕，其中比较知名的影片有《春光乍泄》《蓝宇》《东宫西宫》《蝴蝶》《刺青》等。

讨论题 Discussion

根据课文内容回答下列问题
(Please answer the following questions based on the text)

1. 爱白网是一个什么样的网站？这个网站的读者和网民对美国加州最高法院裁定同性婚姻合法有什么样的反应？
2. 为什么中国的大部分同性恋者仍然戴着面具生活？他们的压力主要来自哪几个方面？
3. 和西方相比，为什么中国社会对同性恋采取了相对宽容的态度？有哪些历史和文化的原因使得中国公众对同性恋的接纳程度比较高？

4. 中国的主流媒体和影视作品对同性恋这个题材采取了什么样的态度？

生词 New Words

1	析		xī	b.f./v.	to analyze, to dissect
2	同性恋	同性戀	tóngxìngliàn	n.	homosexuality
3	最高法院		zuìgāo fǎyuàn	n.p.	supreme court
4	裁定		cáidìng	v.	to rule, to judge, to adjudicate
5	同性		tóngxìng	attr.	the same sex, homosexual
6	基于	基於	jīyú	prep.	because of, in view of, based on
7	裁决	裁決	cáijué	v.	to judge, to adjudicate
8	市政厅	市政廳	shìzhèngtīng	n.	city hall
9	司法官		sīfǎguān	n.	judiciary, law officer
10	仪式	儀式	yíshì	n.	ceremony, rite, function
11	双性恋	雙性戀	shuāngxìngliàn	n.	bisexuality
12	留言		liúyán	v.o./n.	to leave comments; message
13	感慨		gǎnkǎi	v./n.	to sigh with emotion; emotional lament
14	依然		yīrán	adv.	still, as before
15	主流		zhǔliú	n.	mainstream
16	禁忌		jìnjì	n./v.	taboo; to avoid, to abstain from
17	压力	壓力	yālì	n.	pressure

18	权威	權威	quánwēi	n.	authority, power and prestige
19	偏见	偏見	piānjiàn	n.	prejudice, bias
20	歧视	歧視	qíshì	v./n.	to discriminate against, to treat with bias; discrimination (against someone)
21	隐匿	隱匿	yǐnnì	v.	to conceal, to hide
22	面具		miànjù	n.	mask
23	生育		shēngyù	v.	to give birth to
24	子女		zǐnǚ	n.	sons and daughters, offspring
25	大逆不道		dànì-búdào	f.e.	to commit high treason
26	范畴	範疇	fànchóu	n.	category, domain, scope
27	羞耻	羞恥	xiūchǐ	adj.	sense of shame, ashamed
28	面子		miànzi	n.	reputation, prestige, face
29	艾滋病		àizībìng	n.	AIDS
30	加深		jiāshēn	v.	to deepen
31	异性恋	異性戀	yìxìngliàn	n.	heterosexuality
32	相对	相對	xiāngduì	adj.	relative, relatively, comparatively
33	残酷	殘酷	cánkù	adj.	cruel, brutal, ruthless
34	迫害		pòhài	v.	to persecute, to torture
35	判		pàn	v./b.f.	to sentence, to judge
36	死刑		sǐxíng	n.	death penalty
37	舆论	輿論	yúlùn	n.	public opinion
38	一向		yíxiàng	adv.	always, all along, the whole time
39	温和	溫和	wēnhé	adj.	gentle, mild
40	接纳	接納	jiēnà	v.	to admit (into an organization), to accept

41	大致		dàzhì	adv.	approximately, roughly, in general
42	记载	記載	jìzǎi	v./n.	to record; record
43	崇尚		chóngshàng	v.	to uphold, to advocate
44	成语	成語	chéngyǔ	n.	idiom
45	典故		diǎngù	n.	classic allusion, literary quotation
46	代名词	代名詞	dàimíngcí	n.	synonym
47	直觉	直覺	zhíjué	n.	intuition
48	评价	評價	píngjià	v./n.	to appraise, to evaluate; evaluation
49	他人		tārén	pr.	others, other people, other person
50	无关	無關	wúguān	v.	to have nothing to do with, to be irrelevant
51	源远流长	源遠流長	yuányuǎn-liúcháng	f.e.	long-standing and well-established, have a long history
52	不屑一顾	不屑一顧	búxièyígù	f.e.	not worth a glance
53	不至于	不至於	búzhìyú	adv.	cannot go so far, be unlikely
54	条文	條文	tiáowén	n.	article, clause
55	率先		shuàixiān	v.	to take the lead, to be the first to do sth.
56	选修	選修	xuǎnxiū	v.	to take as an elective course
57	名义	名義	míngyì	n.	in the name of
58	频道	頻道	píndào	n.	channel, frequency channel
59	题材	題材	tícái	n.	subject matter, theme
60	访谈	訪談	fǎngtán	v.	to interview
61	栏目	欄目	lánmù	n.	heading or title of a column in a newspaper or magazine, etc.
62	拉拉		lālā	n.	lesbian
63	制作	製作	zhìzuò	v.	to make, to manufacture to, produce

64	访	訪	fǎng	b.f.	visit, call on
65	求助		qiúzhù	v.	to seek help, to ask sb. for help
66	热线	熱線	rèxiàn	n.	hotline (communications link)
67	语	語	yǔ	b.f./v.	language, tongue; to speak
68	读物	讀物	dúwù	n.	reading material
69	华语	華語	Huáyǔ	n.	Chinese language
70	银幕	銀幕	yínmù	n.	screen

专有名词 Proper nouns

1	加利福尼亚	加利福尼亞	Jiālìfúníyà	California
2	加州		Jiāzhōu	California
3	谢汉兰	謝漢蘭	Xiè Hànlán	a person's name
4	旧金山	舊金山	Jiùjīnshān	San Francisco
5	爱白网	愛白網	Àibái Wǎng	a Chinese gay and lesbian website
6	春秋		Chūnqiū	the Spring and Autumn Period (772-481B.C.)
7	战国	戰國	Zhànguó	Warring States Period (476-221B.C.)
8	中央电视台	中央電視臺	Zhōngyāng Diànshìtái	China Central Television (CCTV)
9	凤凰卫视	鳳凰衛視	Fènghuáng Wèishì	Phoenix Satellite Television Channel
10	鲁豫	魯豫	Lǔyù	a person's name
11	春光乍泄		Chūnguāng Zhà Xiè	Happy Together
12	蓝宇	藍宇	Lányǔ	Lan Yu
13	东宫西宫	東宮西宮	Dōnggōng Xīgōng	East Palace, West Palace

| 14 | 蝴蝶 | Húdié | Butterfly |
| 15 | 刺青 | Cìqīng | Tattoo |

词语注释 Vocabulary and Grammar explanations

语素 (morphemes)

-恋：爱、恋爱。(to love; to long for)

> 例　同性恋　双性恋　姐弟恋　自恋　异国恋　单恋　师生恋　三角恋

跨-：超越界限、越过。(to stride; to cross; trans-)

> 例　跨性别　跨国公司　跨年度　跨省　跨区　跨时代　跨界　跨领域
> 　　跨海

非-：不是。(not)

> 例　非主流　非物质文化遗产　非公有　非暴力　非正式　非金属
> 　　非法　非处方药　非卖品　非再生资源　非条件反射

-感：感觉。(feelings)

> 例　羞耻感　荣誉感　口感　美感　归属感　方向感　饥饿感　语感
> 　　满足感　节奏感　幸福感　喜感

-意识：思想、认识、意念。(consciousness)

> 例　群体意识　集体意识　人权意识　民主意识　性意识　危机意思
> 　　忧患意识

24

-心：心理、思想、感情。(heart; state of mind)

> 例　平常心　自尊心　好奇心　野心　耐心　粗心　善心　狠心　进取心
> 　　民心　军心　上进心　童心　雄心　自信心

● 四字格和成语 (four-character expressions and idioms)

● 大逆不道

逆：叛逆；道：封建道德；不道：违反封建道德。原意指破坏封建秩序、违反封建道德的行为。现也用来指不合那些普遍接受的社会观念和道德标准的行为。

("逆" means "rebellious" and "道" means "feudal morality or ethic rules", so "不道" means "rebellion to the feudal rules or impudent insubordination"; now the whole idiom also refers to "an act or behavior that violates all the established social norms, moral rules, and values".)

> （1）由于同性恋无法生育子女，因而属于"大逆不道"的范畴。
> （2）你忘掉自己是什么身分了？竟然敢说出如此大逆不道的话来！
> （3）他从来不听父母的劝告，真是大逆不道！
> （4）在古代，女子私自与男人定婚是大逆不道的行为。

● 不屑一顾

不屑：不值得、不愿意；顾：看。认为不值得一看，形容极端轻视。("不屑" means "not worthy" or "not willing"; "顾" means "to see or look at". The whole idiom means "it is not worth a single glance" or "it is not worthy of serious consideration", indicating extreme contempt.)

(1) 人们对于非主流文化往往采取**不屑一顾**的态度，而不至于残酷迫害它。
(2) 他**不屑一顾**地看了一眼这些礼物，转身离开了。
(3) 他很傲慢，对我们提供的这些帮助**不屑一顾**。
(4) 在别人眼里很宝贵的东西，他从来都**不屑一顾**。

● 虚词及句型 (function words and sentence patterns)

● 既然……就…… since..., then...

固定搭配，多用于书面语。用在因果复句里，前一分句提出已为现实的或已经肯定的原因或理由，后一分句推出结论。"既然"可用在主语前，也可用于主语后。

This is a fixed expression, mostly used in written language. It often occurs in cause-effect complex sentences and means "given the fact that something has been done, something is already the way it is, or a presupposition has been confirmed", which is indicated in the first clause, "then a certain conclusion can be drawn accordingly" in the second clause. "既然" can appear before or after the subject.

(1) 大部分中国人往往以平常心和直觉来评价人与事，认为同性恋**既然**不会伤害他人，**就**与他人无关。
(2) 你**既然**已经来了，**就**把事做完再走吧!
(3) **既然**留学带来的好处如此巨大，我们**就**应当鼓励留学。
(4) **既然**你的病还没好，那**就**不必参加今天的会议了。

● 同……有关 be related to

固定搭配，表示跟某人某事有关系。书面的表达是"与……有关"，否定形式是"与……无关"。"有关"一般用在句末做谓语，不能带宾语。

This is a fixed expression that indicates relationships between people or things. Its more classical expression is "与……有关", and its negative form is "同……无关"."有关" usually occurs at the end of a sentence to function as the predicate, so it cannot take an object.

(1) 这种态度也许同中国人的民族性格有关。
(2) 这次事故同环境污染有关。
(3) 我想借这本图画书，因为我的新工作同儿童教育有关。
(4) 你的病同你吸烟有关，你还是戒烟吧！

- 被……所……　to be done by...

固定搭配，表示被动，用于书面语，更为书面的表达是"为……所……"。"被"和"为"都是介词，引出动作的发出者，动词必须是及物动词。一般来说，如果主要动词是多音节的，"所"可用也可不用；如果主要动词是单音节的，"所"必须用。

This is a fixed passive expression, and its more classical form is "为……所……";"被" and "为" are prepositions and are used to introduce the agent, and their main verb must be a transitive verb. In general, if the main verb is multisyllabic, "所" is optional; however, if the main verb is monosyllabic, "所" is obligatory.

(1) 中国文化源远流长，中国人对自己的主流文化很有信心，从不担心被非主流的文化所影响。
(2) 这种产品的价格一直被几家大公司所垄断。
(3) 他做的很多事情都不被大家（所）理解和认可。
(4) 学生们都被老师的真诚和热情所感动。

- **对于** to; for; about; with regard to; on

介词，引进对待的对象或事物的关系者，相当于"对"。可以和名词、动词和分句组合。用在句子的主语前或后都可以。

This is a preposition used to introduce the person or thing involved in an event, and is similar to "对". It can be combined with nouns, verbs, and clauses and can occur before or after the subject of a sentence.

(1) 对于同性恋，中国没有明确的法律条文加以禁止。
(2) 这本书对于教文学的老师来说帮助非常大。
(3) 对于你提出的问题，我现在还没有答案。
(4) 对于一个学生来说，学习是最重要的事。

副课文 Supplementary Text

同性恋在美国

2004年5月16日，像歌迷排队抢购演唱会门票一样，无数同性伴侣蜂拥而至，提前数小时在美国马萨诸塞州剑桥市府厅外等候登记结婚。2012年5月16日，奥巴马总统在接受美国广播公司采访的时候，宣布他个人支持同性恋结婚。这是美国首位在任总统在同性恋问题上做出如此明确的声明。民意调查显示，美国民众对同性恋的态度较之前发生了重大转变。最近公布的一项盖洛普民意调查结果显示，2015年美国同性婚姻支持率创下历史新高。盖洛普发现，60%的受访者认为，同性伴侣之间的婚姻应该得到法律认可，37%的受访者表示反对；而在1996年，只有27%的美国人支持同性恋，68%的人持反对态度。在同性婚姻的问题上，从2004年美国第一对同性伴侣在马萨诸塞州结婚到今天，同性婚姻已经扩展到全美37个州和首都华盛顿。美国联邦最高法院在2015年6月底就是否使同性婚姻在全美合法化的问题作了判决，承认了同性婚姻的合法性。

美国社会对同性恋经历了从迫害、漠视到宽容的漫长历程。要想让游离于文化主流之外的同性恋亚文化被全美国所接受是非常不容易的。以下几点是美国人不能真正接受同性恋文化的主要原因：

一、根深蒂固的宗教信仰

欧美社会反对同性恋的一个主要原因可归结于《圣经》对他们的洗礼。《圣经》里提到，婚姻必须是一男一女的结合。上帝创造男人和女人，男人和女人可以生下小孩。同性恋不能繁衍后代，这就违背了上帝的造人原则。美国是一个以基督教为根基的国家，生活在这片土地的人们当然也依傍这样的准则世世代代地繁衍着生命。

二、无形之手——政治影响

为了在竞选中争取更多的选票，美国的共和党和民主党对同性恋采取了不同态度。较为保守的共和党，其主要支持者——中产阶级及富人大多是观念比较传统的人，为此，共和党的态度以反对为主；而支持者主要为妇女、少数族裔、低收入人群的民主党则相对开放。这样一支无形之手，势必影响着美国社会对同性恋文化的认可度。

三、"艾滋病"传播的替罪羊

在80年代，在同性恋者身上验出首例艾滋病。不管是由于部分同性恋者的不检点，还是部分保守人士的故意误导所致，总之，给公众造成了"同性恋者=艾滋病"的错误观念。艾滋病不仅给个人造成了损失和伤害，还再次引发了公众对同性恋者的歧视和排斥。虽然，现今医学证实，滥交才容易导致艾滋病，同性恋者和艾滋病没有必然联系，但其对同性恋者的负面影响仍未消除，甚至扩散到全球。

四、主流下的阴霾——亚文化

从古至今，男女相配永远是占据主流的思想，后期兴起的同性恋思潮不能与主流思想相抗衡。因此，同性恋文化要想在主流思潮下求生存是难上加难的事情。

尽管以上列举了许多美国同性恋文化发展已经遇到或将会遇到的困难，它还是蓬勃地滋长着。我们看到了社会对它的认可，因为每一个人都有权利追寻自己的自由和幸福。

讨论题 Discussion

根据课文内容回答下列问题
(Please answer the following questions based on the text)

1. 美国社会对同性恋的态度怎么样？
2. 《圣经》对婚姻的看法是什么？
3. 美国政治党派对同性恋有什么影响？
4. 同性恋和艾滋病有什么关系？
5. 相对于主流文化，作者认为同性恋属于什么文化范畴？
6. 请你分析一下你们国家或地区的同性恋文化和现状。

生词 New Words

1	歌迷		gēmí	n.	fan
2	排队	排隊	pái duì	v.o.	to queue up, to line up
3	抢购	搶購	qiǎnggòu	v.	to rush to purchase
4	演唱会	演唱會	yǎnchànghuì	n.	vocal concert

5	门票	門票	ménpiào	n.	entrance ticket, admission ticket
6	蜂拥而至	蜂擁而至	fēngyōng-érzhì	f.e.	to stream in
7	市府		shìfǔ	n.	municipal government
8	厅	廳	tīng	b.f./n.	hall
9	等候		děnghòu	v.	to wait
10	声明	聲明	shēngmíng	v./n.	to announce; statement, declaration
11	公布	公佈	gōngbù	v.	to promulgate, to announce, to publish
12	率		lǜ	n./b.f.	rate, ratio
13	受访者	受訪者	shòufǎngzhě	n.	interviewee
14	扩展	擴展	kuòzhǎn	v.	to expand, to broaden, to spread
15	月底		yuèdǐ	n.	the end of a month
16	判决	判決	pànjué	n./v.	court decision, judgment; to sentence
17	漫长	漫長	màncháng	adj.	very long, extensive, endless
18	历程	歷程	lìchéng	n.	course, process
19	游离	游離	yóulí	v.	to drift away, to dissociate
20	之外		zhīwài	n.	being excluded; besides, except, beyond
21	根深蒂固		gēnshēn-dìgù	f.e.	deep-rooted, inveterate
22	归结	歸結	guījié	v.	to sum up
23	洗礼	洗禮	xǐlǐ	n.	baptism
24	提到		tídào	v(c)	to mention, to refer to
25	小孩		xiǎohái	n.	child, kid
26	繁衍		fányǎn	v.	to multiply, to increase gradually in number or quantity
27	后代	後代	hòudài	n.	descendants, posterity
28	违背	違背	wéibèi	v.	to violate, to go against
29	根基		gēnjī	n.	foundation, basis
30	依傍		yībàng	v.	to rely upon, to depend on

#	简体	繁體	Pinyin	POS	English
31	准则	準則	zhǔnzé	n.	norm, standard, criterion
32	世世代代		shìshì-dàidài	f.e.	for generations, age after age
33	无形	無形	wúxíng	attr.	invisible, intangible
34	竞选	競選	jìngxuǎn	v.	to enter into an election, to campaign, to run for
35	选票	選票	xuǎnpiào	n.	vote, ballot
36	保守		bǎoshǒu	adj.	conservative
37	中产阶级	中產階級	zhōngchǎn jiējí	n.p.	middle class
38	大多		dàduō	adv.	for the most part, many, most
39	为此	為此	wèicǐ	adv.	for this reason, therefore
40	势必	勢必	shìbì	adv.	certainly will, be bound to
41	替罪羊		tìzuìyáng	n.	scapegoat
42	验	驗	yàn	v.	to inspect, to examine, to check
43	检点	檢點	jiǎndiǎn	v.	to be cautious or restrained
44	误导	誤導	wùdǎo	v.	to mislead, to lead astray, to misguide
45	致		zhì	v.	to result in
46	再次		zàicì	adv.	second time, once more
47	排斥		páichì	v.	to exclude, to repel
48	现今	現今	xiànjīn	n.	nowadays
49	证实	證實	zhèngshí	v.	to confirm, to verify
50	滥交	濫交	lànjiāo	v./n.	to have a casual sex; promiscuity
51	消除		xiāochú	v.	to eliminate, to dispel, to remove
52	扩散	擴散	kuòsàn	v.	to spread, to diffuse, to proliferate
53	占据	佔據	zhànjù	v.	to occupy, to hold
54	后期	後期	hòuqī	n.	later stage, later period
55	兴起	興起	xīngqǐ	v.	to rise, to spring up
56	思潮		sīcháo	n.	trend of thought

57	抗衡		kànghéng	v.	to compete, to counterweight
58	列举	列舉	lièjǔ	v.	to list
59	滋长	滋長	zīzhǎng	v.	to grow, to develop

专有名词 Proper nouns

1	马萨诸塞	馬薩諸塞	Mǎsàzhūsài	Massachusetts
2	剑桥	劍橋	Jiànqiáo	Cambridge
3	奥巴马	奧巴馬	Àobāmǎ	Obama
4	美国广播公司	美國廣播公司	Měiguó Guǎngbō Gōngsī	American Broadcasting Company (ABC)
5	盖洛普	蓋洛普	Gàiluòpǔ	Gallup, Inc.
6	圣经	聖經	Shèngjīng	the Bible
7	上帝		Shàngdì	God
8	民主党	民主黨	Mínzhǔdǎng	Democratic Party

第3课 3D打印与未来生活

主课文 Main Text

煎饼，生活常见的街边小吃；3D打印，高大上的前沿技术，将两者结合在一起会是什么样子呢？最近，国外网站 Kickstarter 就亮相了一台3D煎饼打印机，堪称煎饼艺术家。它自带面糊容器和烤盘，而且做到了完全自动。该打印机需要一个配套软件来完成煎饼形状的设计，然后用存储卡将图片从电脑复制到打印机中，就可以坐吃煎饼了。

3D打印也就是人们常说的增材制造，即利用数字文件通过3D打印机制造3D实物的先进制造和设计流程。在最近这几年里，3D打印已经成为科技产业当中非常重要的一股力量，被广泛应用于国防、航空航天、生物医药、土木工程等领域。或许你会觉得3D打印距离你的生活还非常遥远，但它却是一种会真正改变我们未来生活的技术。小到一颗螺丝，大到一幢房子，3D打印似乎"无所不能"，一个新兴的数字生产革命已悄然来临。

英国剑桥大学研究人员用3D技术来修复老鼠的视网膜细胞，美国的企业用3D技术制出了金属枪，日本警视厅利用3D打印技术还原作案现场，破获了一起重大杀人案。据英国《每日邮报》12月7日报道，3D技术成功地打印出了美国总统奥巴马的塑像。一对80后建筑师夫妇在设计他们的婚礼中也用到了3D打印技术。他们认为3D打印并不是高高在上、遥不可及的东西，它完全可以和生活融合在一起。比如说在他们的这场婚礼中所用到的灯具、喜糖盒、筷子、首饰，甚至包括结婚戒指、手捧花、婚纱等等全部都是由他们自己设计并由3D打印制成的。3D打印技术的发展为人们的生活开启了一扇通往无限可能的大门。

3D打印在医疗领域最常见的用途之一就是制作骨头、软骨的替代品，以及医疗设备。这方面的应用已经取得了很大进展。目前，美国动物保护组织利用3D打印技术制作假肢，让一只左脚畸形的小白鸭生平第一次能够正常行走。毛毛是一只有先天性残疾的小白鸭，它的左脚生下来就长错了方向，是向后而非向前的。因为左脚严重畸形，毛毛无法正常行走，当它走路时，脚部会疼痛不已甚至发生感染，带来致命性的后果。毛毛畸形的左脚被切除后，3D打印公司Novacopy，用柔软耐用的硅胶为毛毛3D打印出一只可以自由活动的左脚。虽然它的步伐还略显蹒跚，但是毛毛依靠硅胶假肢已能如其他鸭子一样正常走路了。

根据一家信息研究和咨询公司最近的报告，3D打印正在快速演变，尽管当中的许多技术距离在主流市场上的普及仍需要五到十年的时间。相比一般消费者，商业和医疗领域对于3D打印技术的采纳速度会更快一些，因为这两个领域当中存在更加迫切的应用需求。与此同时，我们将会看到更多优质的新材料出现，3D打印机的速度也将会得到提升。由于在制作物品上的便捷性，3D打印机也将越来越多地出现在课堂上。在个体消费者市场准备好要腾飞之时，我们可能还会看到苹果、亚马逊或谷歌推出自己的3D打印机。

讨论题 Discussion

根据课文内容回答下列问题
(Please answer the following questions based on the text):

1. 什么是3D打印？3D打印现在已经被用于哪些领域中？
2. 文章中的那对80后建筑师夫妇对3D打印技术怎么看？他们用3D打印做出了哪些东西？
3. 3D打印在医疗领域最常见的用途是什么？美国动物保护组织利用3D打印技术给小白鸭毛毛制作了什么？
4. 在作者看来，哪些领域对于3D打印技术的采纳速度会更快一些？为什么？
5. 作者预测在个体消费者市场对3D技术有需求时，哪些公司会尽快推出自己的3D打印机？

生词 New Words

1	打印		dǎyìn	v.	to print
2	煎饼	煎餅	jiānbing	n.	pancake
3	小吃	小喫	xiǎochī	n.	snack, refreshments
4	前沿		qiányán	n.	cutting-edge, frontline, front edge
5	亮相		liàng xiàng	v.o.	to strike a pose on stage, to debut
6	堪		kān	aux.	may, can
7	面糊	麵糊	miànhù	n.	flour paste
8	容器		róngqì	n.	container, receptacle, vessel

9	配套		pèi tào	v.o.	to match, to form a complete set
10	存储	存儲	cúnchǔ	v.	to store, to keep
11	复制	複製	fùzhì	v.	to duplicate, to reproduce
12	材		cái	n.	material
13	实物	實物	shíwù	n.	material object
14	流程		liúchéng	n.	manufacturing, technological process
15	当中	當中	dāngzhōng	n.	among
16	国防	國防	guófáng	n.	national defense
17	航天		hángtiān	n.	aerospace, cosmonautics
18	医药	醫藥	yīyào	n.	medicine
19	土木工程		tǔmù gōngchéng	n.p.	civil engineering
20	螺丝	螺絲	luósī	n.	screw
21	幢		zhuàng	m(n)	measure word for houses
22	无所不能	無所不能	wúsuǒbùnéng	f.e.	omnipotent, almighty
23	悄然		qiǎorán	adv.	quietly, softly, noiselessly
24	来临	來臨	láilín	v.	to arrive, to come, to approach
25	修复	修復	xiūfù	v.	to repair, to restore
26	老鼠		lǎoshǔ	n.	mouse, rat
27	视网膜	視網膜	shìwǎngmó	n.	retinal
28	细胞	細胞	xìbāo	n.	cell
29	制	製	zhì	v.	to make, to manufacture, to produce
30	还原	還原	huán yuán	v.o.	to return to the original condition/shape
31	作案		zuò àn	v.o.	to commit a crime or an offense

32	破获	破獲	pòhuò	v.	to crack a case and capture the criminal, to uncover (a criminal plot)
33	塑像		sùxiàng	n.	statue
34	夫妇	夫婦	fūfù	n.	husband and wife, married couple
35	婚礼	婚禮	hūnlǐ	n.	wedding ceremony, wedding
36	高高在上		gāogāo-zàishàng	f.e.	be far from the masses and reality, be high above
37	遥不可及	遙不可及	yáobùkějí	f.e.	out of reach
38	融合		rónghé	v.	to mix together, to fuse; assimilation, fusion
39	灯具	燈具	dēngjù	n.	lamp
40	喜糖		xǐtáng	n.	candies or sweets for entertaining friends and relatives at a wedding
41	首饰	首飾	shǒushì	n.	jewelry
42	戒指		jièzhi	n.	ring
43	婚纱	婚紗	hūnshā	n.	wedding dress, bridal veil
44	开启	開啟	kāiqǐ	v.	to open, to initiate
45	扇		shàn	m(n)	measure word for doors or windows
46	通往		tōngwǎng	v.	to lead to
47	用途		yòngtú	n.	use, purpose, application
48	软骨	軟骨	ruǎngǔ	n.	cartilage
49	替代		tìdài	v.	to substitute for, to replace; substitution
50	品		pǐn	b.f.	article, product
51	日前		rìqián	n.	a few days ago, the other day
52	假肢		jiǎzhī	n.	artificial limb
53	脚	腳	jiǎo	n.	foot

54	畸形		jīxíng	adj.	deformity, malformation, abnormal
55	鸭	鴨	yā	n	duck
56	生平		shēngpíng	n.	ever since one's birth; one's entire life
57	行走		xíngzǒu	v.	to walk, to go about
58	先天		xiāntiān	n./attr.	congenital, inborn, inherent
59	残疾	殘疾	cánjí	n.	disability, handicap
60	走路		zǒu lù	v.o.	to walk, to go on foot
61	疼痛		téngtòng	adj.	ache, painful
62	不已		bùyǐ	v.	to be endless, endlessly, incessantly
63	感染		gǎnrǎn	v.	to infect
64	致命		zhìmìng	attr./v.	fatal, mortal, lethal; to cause death
65	后果	後果	hòuguǒ	n.	consequence, aftermath
66	切除		qiēchú	v.	to resect, to cut off
67	柔软	柔軟	róuruǎn	adj.	soft
68	硅胶	硅膠	guījiāo	n.	silica gel
69	步伐		bùfá	n.	pace, (measured) step
70	显	顯	xiǎn	v.	to show, to display, to manifest
71	蹒跚	蹣跚	pánshān	v.	to dodder, to stagger, to stumble
72	演变	演變	yǎnbiàn	v.	to develop, to evolve
73	普及		pǔjí	v.	to popularize, to disseminate, to spread
74	采纳	採納	cǎinà	v.	to accept, to adopt
75	需求		xūqiú	n.	demand, need
76	优质	優質	yōuzhì	adj.	high (or top) quality, high grade

77	便捷		biànjié	adj.	direct and simple, convenient, easy
78	课堂	課堂	kètáng	n.	classroom
79	腾飞	騰飛	téngfēi	v.	to fly swiftly upward, to soar
80	推出		tuīchū	v(c)	to present to the public, to release

专有名词 Proper nouns

1	剑桥大学	劍橋大學	Jiànqiáo Dàxué	University of Cambridge
2	日本警视厅	日本警視廳	Rìběn Jǐngshìtīng	Japan's National Police Agency
3	每日邮报	每日郵報	Měirì Yóubào	*Daily Mail*
4	亚马逊	亞馬遜	Yàmǎxùn	Amazon
5	谷歌		Gǔgē	Google

词语注释 Vocabulary and Grammar explanations

语素 (morphemes)

-家： 掌握某种专门学识或从事某种工作、有较高成就的人。
(expert; specialist in a certain field)

> 例　艺术家　作家　画家　科学家　音乐家　舞蹈家　化学家　数学家
> 　　军事学家　历史学家　医学家　考古学家

-卡： 用于记录某种信息的薄片状物体。(card)

> 例　存储卡　信用卡　饭卡　学生卡　门卡　图书卡　银行卡　电话卡

复-：再。(again)

> 例　复制　复习　复印　复发　复婚　复信　复试　复学　复工

-具：用具；器械。(utensil; tool; appliance)

> 例　灯具　玩具　茶具　家具　工具　厨具　文具　办公用具

-品：物件。(article ; product)

> 例　替代品　用品　物品　赠品　装饰品　化妆品　奢侈品　食品　商品

-域：范围。(domain; scope)

> 例　领域　海域　地域　界域　疆域　空域

● 四字格和成语 (four-character expressions and idioms)

● 无所不能

　　无所：没有什么。无所不能：没有什么不能做的，指什么都能做。(omnipotent or capable of doing anything)

> 例　无所不能　无所不知　无所畏惧　无所不谈

> 例　(1) 3D打印似乎"无所不能"，一个新兴的数字生产革命已悄然来临。
> (2) 说起机器人，大家都觉得它们无所不能，能够帮助人类解决所有困难。
> (3) 诸葛亮 (Zhuge Liang) 以智谋被后世传颂，他上知天文下知地理，几乎无所不能。
> (4) 在孩子心中，父亲看上去高大魁梧、无所不能。

- **高高在上**

    离大众很远，或跟实际不相符合。(to be far from the masses and reality)

    (1) 他们认为 3D 打印并不是高高在上、遥不可及的东西，它完全可以和生活融合在一起。
    (2) 明星总是给人一种高高在上的感觉。
    (3) 最近有媒体报道，原来高高在上的星级酒店推出了自助餐外卖服务。
    (4) 谈到私人飞机，大多数人可能都会觉得它高高在上，遥不可及。

- **遥不可及**

    指非常遥远、难以得到。(very far; out of reach)

    (1) 他们认为 3D 打印并不是高高在上、遥不可及的东西，它完全可以和生活融合在一起。
    (2) 科学家正在寻找另一个地球，但是那似乎是一个遥不可及的美丽童话。
    (3) 专家声称人类想要长生不死并不是那么遥不可及。
    (4) 对于大多数普通百姓来说，买房，尤其在一线城市买房，依然是遥不可及的梦想。

- **疼痛不已**

    不已：不停止 (endlessly; incessantly)。疼痛不已：指疼痛不停止。(the pain does not stop)

    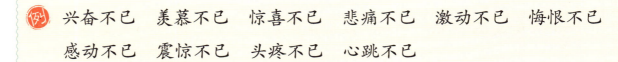

（1）毛毛无法正常行走，当它走路时，脚部会疼痛不已甚至发生感染，带来致命性的后果。

（2）中国经济发展的速度之快让世界震惊不已。

（3）外婆的去世让他悲痛不已。

（4）苹果的新产品太酷了，粉丝们兴奋不已。

虚词及句型 (function words and sentence patterns)

• 该 this; that; the above-mentioned

代词，指前面说过的人或事物，相当于"这个"或者"那个"，可指人，也可指事物，做定语，用于书面语。

This is a pronoun that refers to the person or thing previously mentioned and is similar to "这个" or "那个" in meaning. It is always used as an attributive to modify nouns and is a written expression.

（1）该打印机需要一个配套软件来完成煎饼形状的设计，然后用存储卡将图片从电脑复制到打印机中，就可以坐吃煎饼了。

（2）他从小就是一个聪明的孩子。学校记录显示该生每门功课的成绩都是A。

（3）Mount Holyoke College建于1837年。该校是一所历史悠久的女子大学。

（4）苹果公司是一家著名的企业。该公司的产品主要是电脑和智能手机。

● **当中 among**

名词。常见的格式是：名词＋当中。表示范围。

This is a fixed expression; the often seen form is: "noun + 当中", indicating the scope of something.

 (1) 在最近这几年里，3D打印已经成为科技产业当中非常重要的一股力量。
(2) 受教育程度在高中以下的成年美国人当中，有三分之一不上网。
(3) 在求职者的学历、经验、专业训练、家庭背景当中，经验和专业训练对用人单位来说更重要。
(4) 在三个姐妹当中，父母最疼爱小女儿。

● **小到……大到…… small to...big to...**

固定搭配。通过列举最小和最大的案例说明范围之广。常用来表示包罗万象，穷尽所有的意思。

This structure is used to provide two extreme cases: the smallest and the biggest. It is usually used to describe inclusiveness of a case, situation, or an organization. It has the meaning of "all-inclusive" and "all-embracing".

 (1) 小到一颗螺丝，大到一幢房子，3D打印似乎"无所不能"，一个新兴的数字生产革命已悄然来临。
(2) 小到日用小商品，大到家用电器，都降价了30%到50%。
(3) 世界上有各种各样的风俗，小到吃穿住行，大到婚俗葬礼，都因地而异，各不相同。
(4) 对于喜欢购物的游客来说，日本几乎可以买到所有你想要的东西，小到本土的药品，大到世界顶级品牌，而且在商场内就可以直接完成退税。

……之一 one of...

固定用法。用于说明一个大类中的一个例子。
This is a fixed expression used to indicate an example in a certain category.

(1) 3D打印在医疗领域最常见的用途之一就制作骨头、软骨的替代品，以及医疗设备。
(2) 加拿大是"七大工业组织"的成员国，是世界工业领袖之一。
(3) 中国是向欧美市场出口产品的主要国家之一。
(4) 中国教育改革的目标之一就是提高学生的创造力和独立思考的能力。

副课文 Supplementary Text

情感慢递店　浪漫寄心情

情侣如果能给爱人写封信，留下对今后的期望和梦想，多年后再打开这封信，回忆当年的情感和宝贵时光，这显然是件浪漫的事。这样的慢递服务如今非常流行，而在南京也有人在快节奏的现代生活中赚起"慢钱"来。老板是一位80后的姑娘，店里的业务是顾客可以给某个人写封信，然后指定未来信件发出的年月日。

80后小店店主"树小姐"提供慢递服务，可以邮寄一张明信片给未来的自己。未来某一天，你就可以收到今天的心情。"树小姐"告诉记者，小店自从2011年12月24日开张起就有了慢递业务，几乎每天都会有人来享受这个服务，有时候一天多至二三十人，到现在为止已经贮藏了几百张将要寄出的明信片了。顾客大多以年轻人、情侣为主。时间最久远的两张明信片出自一对情侣之手。他们相约十年后再接收来自彼此的心情和真实感受，以见证他们的爱情。小店接待过最年长的顾客是一位已过花甲之年的老奶奶，她特地来店里挑了一张明信片寄给自己的小孙女，希望孙女长大后能收到自己满满的爱与鼓励。

慢递服务让"树小姐"交上了不少朋友。顾客很多都不是本地人，他们往往在南京逗留了一段时间之后就各奔东西。然而与"树小姐"熟识后，身在各地的顾客也不忘给她寄上一张明信片，表达对生活的美好向往与祝愿。

"树小姐"说，她的顾客多是回头客，"因为每段时间自己的心情不同，所以大家在收到慢递后又会再写新的，所以我和大部分顾客都成了好朋友"。"有那么多朋友都在想着你，关心着你，这本身就是一件多么幸福的事啊"。

慢递是一种和普通邮局相同的信件投递服务，唯一的区别是，投递的时间由寄信人自己决定。这样的慢递店与快递店不同的不只是递送的速度，而且还契合了都市人不同的心理需求。在时间就是效率的今天，快递公司由于符合上班族高效率的工作特点，生意越来越火。但是快节奏的生活使人感到压抑，产生焦虑感。另外，物质的繁荣和对物质的狂热追求，必定导致情感的空虚。人们需要找到情感的发泄口，诉诸自己内心的真实感情。以慢递为代表的情感消费可在一定程度上满足这一需求。慢递以一种类似行为艺术的方式，提醒人们在快速发展的现代社会中去关注自己的当下，目前在上海、北京等大城市已开始流行。

讨论题 Discussion

阅读以后请回答下列问题
(Please answer the following questions based on the text)

1. "慢递"是什么样的服务？你对这样的服务有什么看法？
2. "树小姐"的店生意怎么样？顾客是什么样的人？他们慢递的是什么？
3. "慢递"这种形式在现代生活中有什么意义？
4. 如果你去"树小姐"的店，会写一封什么样的信？为什么？
5. 在"分秒必争"的现代生活压力下，你用什么方式使你的生活慢下来？

生词 New Words

#					
1	期望		qīwàng	v./n.	to hope, to expect; expectation
2	梦想	夢想	mèngxiǎng	n./v.	dream, illusion, fantasy; to dream
3	打开	打開	dǎkāi	v(c)	to break open, to undo, to open
4	节奏	節奏	jiézòu	n.	rhythm, pace
5	赚	賺	zhuàn	v.	to make a profit, to gain, to earn (money)
6	指定		zhǐdìng	v.	to appoint, to specify, to designate
7	信件		xìnjiàn	n.	letter, mail
8	邮寄	郵寄	yóujì	v.	to mail, to post
9	明信片		míngxìnpiàn	n.	postcard
10	开张	開張	kāi zhāng	v.o.	to open a business
11	贮藏	貯藏	zhùcáng	v.	to store
12	久远	久遠	jiǔyuǎn	adj.	far back, ages ago
13	相约	相約	xiāngyuē	v.	to agree, to reach agreement
14	接收		jiēshōu	v.	to receive, to accept
15	见证	見證	jiànzhèng	v./n.	to witness; testimony
16	花甲		huājiǎ	n.	a cycle of sixty years, sixty years of age
17	特地		tèdì	adv.	for a special purpose, specially
18	孙女	孫女	sūnnǚ	n.	son's daughter, granddaughter
19	逗留		dòuliú	v.	to stay, to stop, to linger
20	奔		bèn	v.	to run quickly, to hurry or rush
21	熟识	熟識	shúshi	v.	be well acquainted with, to know well

22	向往	向往	xiàngwǎng	v.	to yearn for, to look forward to
23	祝愿	祝願	zhùyuàn	v.	to wish
24	回头客	回頭客	huítóukè	n.	returned customer
25	投递	投遞	tóudì	v.	to deliver, to send
26	区别	區別	qūbié	v./n.	to distinguish, to differentiate; difference
27	契合		qìhé	v.	to agree with, to tally with
28	效率		xiàolǜ	n.	efficiency
29	压抑	壓抑	yāyì	v.	to constrain, to inhibit, to depress
30	焦虑	焦慮	jiāolǜ	adj.	worry
31	繁荣	繁榮	fánróng	adj.	flourishing, prosperous, booming
32	狂热	狂熱	kuángrè	adj.	fanatic, fanatical, feverish, mad
33	空虚		kōngxū	adj.	hollow, empty
34	发泄	發洩	fāxiè	v.	to give vent to, to let off
35	诉诸	訴諸	sùzhū	v.	to resort to
36	类似	類似	lèisì	v.	to be analogous, to be similar
37	当下	當下	dāngxià	n./adv.	current or present situation; at once, immediately, presently

专有名词 Proper nouns

| 南京 | | Nánjīng | Nanjing (capital of Jiangsu Province) |

在线大学：在网络时代实现"有教无类"的梦想

第 4 课

主课文 Main Text

中国的思想家、教育家孔子在两千多年前提出了"有教无类"的教育理念。这个理念有超越时代的意义，主张"在教育面前人人平等"。两千多年来，"教育不分贫富、种族、性别和年龄"一直是人类的梦想；而在现实生活中仍有千千万万的人由于种种原因被关在高等学府的大门之外。

近年来，在线大学"慕课"（MOOC）的兴办又一次张起了"教育平等""精英教育平民化"的大旗。通过网络，免费学习全球知名大学的课程正在成为一种新型的学习模式。这场席卷全球的"慕课教学实践"使世界上最优质的教育传播到地球最偏远的角落，也让"随时随地"的终身学习不再遥远。《时代周刊》记者阿曼达·里普利这样写道："慕课提供者将褪去高等教育的所有浮华外衣——品牌、价格，还有设施，让我们所有人记起教育的本质是学习。"2012年11月比尔·盖茨基金会向世界上最大的在线学习首创机构edX

投资一百万美元。在比尔·盖茨看来，发展在线教育的必要性就在于"高等教育的成本很高，人们持续学习的需求也很强烈；同时，教育质量也没有达到我们想要的高度"。edX的首席执行主管Anant Agarwal在2014年的一次媒体采访中表示："我们坚信，我们可以为所有地方的所有人提供真正的顶级在线课程，不论其社会地位如何或者收入多少；与此同时，我们也力图改善学校教育质量。"

哪些人已经受益于这种新型的教育方式呢？中国山东大学生刘磊厌倦了死板的"老师念笔记，学生记笔记"的授课方式，于是就在他钟爱的"果壳网"的"慕课自习室"里选修了一门Udacity的生物课，因此拥有了肤色各异的两万多名同学。他每天坐在宿舍里，看着视频上的美国教授和十几个学生或侃侃而谈、或激烈争论，时不时提交自己的见解，学得兴趣盎然。年仅十七岁的巴图辛·米昂甘巴雅是麻省理工学院一年级学生，来自蒙古国。他之所以有机会入读美国名校，完全得益于"慕课"。两年前，他在网上注册了麻省理工学院的大学二年级水平的"电路和电子学"课程，当时年方十五岁的巴图辛在这门课上成绩优异，让麻省理工学院刮目相看，向他发出了入学通知书。美国伊利诺伊州民主党人、参议员理查德·杜尔宾注册了一门"现代美国诗歌"的网络课程。还有一位上同一课程的学生是常年卧病在床的八十一岁希腊老人，他还在网络上发表了关于诗人艾米莉·迪金森的研究论文。

"慕课"教学在诸多方面冲击着传统的高等教育模式。它不仅向全球免费提供知名高校的优质课程，而且正在通过课堂与在线混合模式重构校园教育。刚从美国回到清华大学的年轻学者徐葳，从伯克利大学带回了一门名为"云计算与软件工程"的在线课程，通过与传统课堂教学结合，使得学习更加深入和个性化，提高了教与学的质量和效率。美国乔治亚理工大学校长乔治·皮特森曾这样表示："'慕课'预示着教育领域有发生颠覆性变革的可能性，向那些每年收五万美元学费的大学提出一个挑战：如果知识可以从互联网免费获得，你得提供什么样的教育才值这个钱？"

在线教育是网络时代的产物，有很多优越性，使我们在"教育平等"和"优质教育平民化"方面迈进了一大步。然而，专家一致认为，"在线教育并不能完全替代传统教育"。在目前的技术背景下，比较适合"慕课"的课程有两类：一是通过文字、视频这种传导方式能够让学生比较容易接受的课程；二是某些虽然复杂一点，甚至需要动手操作，但可以通过逻辑或者代码学习的一些课程。真正凭借自身体验和老师直接指导的课程，还要依靠课堂教育。更重要的是，有些东西，你只能在场才能获得。传统课堂教育中深度探讨、动手实践、与老师同学互动等特质是在线教育无法提供的。另外，在线课程目前还有很多问题，比如教师缺乏动力、学生参与程度低、课程完成率不理想、学习效果缺乏权威性检验等，都是有待完善、解决的。

讨论题 Discussion

根据课文内容回答下列问题

(Please answer the following questions based on the text)：

1. "有教无类"是什么样的教育理念？
2. "慕课"教育有哪些优势？它能实现"有教无类"的梦想吗？
3. "慕课"教育对哪些人会有很大的帮助？为什么？
4. "慕课"教育在哪些方面会冲击传统教育？为什么？
5. 为什么在线教育不能完全代替传统教育？
6. 你对在线教育有什么看法？

生词 New Words

1	有教无类	有教無類	yǒujiào-wúlèi	f.e.	to provide education to all people without discrimination
2	超越		chāoyuè	v.	to surpass, to transcend, to go beyond
3	贫富	貧富	pínfù	n.	the poor and the rich

4	种族	種族	zhǒngzú	n.	race (of people)
5	千千万万	千千萬萬	qiānqiān-wànwàn	r.f.	thousands upon thousands
6	高等		gāoděng	attr.	higher, advanced, high-level
7	学府	學府	xuéfǔ	n.	institution of higher learning
8	慕课	慕課	mùkè	n.	Mooc, Massive Open Online Course
9	兴办	興辦	xīngbàn	v.	to start, to initiate, to set up
10	精英		jīngyīng	n.	elite
11	平民		píngmín	n.	ordinary people, civilian
12	旗		qí	n.	flag, banner
13	免费	免費	miǎnfèi	v.o.	to be free of charge
14	新型		xīnxíng	attr.	new type, new pattern
15	席卷	席捲	xíjuǎn	v.	to roll up like a mat, to engulf, to sweep
16	偏远	偏遠	piānyuǎn	adj.	remote, faraway
17	角落		jiǎoluò	n.	corner, remote place
18	随地	隨地	suídì	adv.	anywhere, in any place
19	终身	終身	zhōngshēn	n.	lifelong, all one's life, lifetime
20	褪		tuì	v.	to take off, to shed, to slip out of sth.
21	浮华	浮華	fúhuá	adj.	flashy, ostentatious, flamboyant
22	外衣		wàiyī	n.	coat, outer garment
23	设施	設施	shèshī	n.	installation, facilities
24	基金会	基金會	jījīnhuì	n.	foundation, board of directors of a fund
25	首席		shǒuxí	n.	chief
26	坚信	堅信	jiānxìn	v.	to firmly believe

27	顶级	頂級	dǐngjí	n.	top level
28	力图	力圖	lìtú	v.	to try hard to, strive to do one's best to
29	受益		shòuyì	v.	to profit by, to benefit from
30	厌倦	厭倦	yànjuàn	v.	to be weary of, to be tired of
31	死板		sǐbǎn	adj.	rigid, inflexible, stiff
32	授课	授課	shòu kè	v.o.	to give lessons, to give instruction
33	钟爱	鍾愛	zhōng'ài	v.	to have a passion for, to be very fond of
34	自习	自習	zìxí	v.	to study by oneself
35	肤色	膚色	fūsè	n.	color of skin
36	异	異	yì	b.f.	different
37	视频	視頻	shìpín	n.	video clips
38	侃侃而谈	侃侃而談	kǎnkǎn-értán	f.e.	to talk with ease and confidence
39	提交		tíjiāo	v.	to submit, to refer to
40	见解	見解	jiànjiě	n.	view, opinion
41	盎然		àngrán	adj.	abundant, full
42	得益		déyì	v.	to receive benefit, to benefit, to profit
43	电路	電路	diànlù	n.	(electric) circuit
44	电子学	電子學	diànzǐxué	n.	electronics
45	优异	優異	yōuyì	adj.	excellent, outstanding
46	刮目相看		guāmù-xiāngkàn	f.e.	to treat a person with increased respect, to look at a person with new eyes
47	入学	入學	rù xué	v.o.	to enroll in a school or college
48	参议员	參議員	cānyìyuán	n.	senator
49	诗歌	詩歌	shīgē	n.	poems and songs, poetry

50	常年		chángnián	n./adv.	throughout the year, all the year round
51	卧病	臥病	wòbìng	v.	to be sick abed
52	诸多	諸多	zhūduō	adj.	a good deal, a lot of
53	混合		hùnhé	v.	to mix, to blend, to mingle
54	构	構	gòu	b.f.	to construct, to form, to build
55	回到		huídào	v(c)	to return to, to go back to
56	学者	學者	xuézhě	n.	scholar, literati
57	预示	預示	yùshì	v.	to forebode, to foreshadow, to betoken
58	颠覆	顛覆	diānfù	v.	to overturn, to overthrow
59	变革	變革	biàngé	v.	to transform, to reform, to change
60	值		zhí	v.	to be worth
61	产物	產物	chǎnwù	n.	outcome, result (of), product
62	优越	優越	yōuyuè	adj.	superior, advantageous
63	迈进	邁進	màijìn	v(c)	to stride forward, to forge ahead
64	传导	傳導	chuándǎo	v.	to transmit, to conduct
65	代码	代碼	dàimǎ	n.	code
66	凭借	憑藉	píngjiè	v.	to depend on, by means of
67	自身		zìshēn	n.	self, oneself
68	在场	在場	zàichǎng	v.	to be present, to be on the scene
69	深度		shēndù	n./adj.	depth; in depth
70	探讨	探討	tàntǎo	v.	to inquire into, to discuss, to probe
71	特质	特質	tèzhì	n.	special quality, characteristics
72	动力	動力	dònglì	n.	motivation, drive, driving force

73	检验	檢驗	jiǎnyàn	v./n.	to test, to examine, to inspect; examination
74	有待		yǒudài	v.	to remain (to be done), to be pending, to await
75	完善		wánshàn	v./adj.	to perfect, to improve; perfect

专有名词 Proper nouns

1	孔子		Kǒngzǐ	Confucius
2	时代周刊	時代週刊	Shídài Zhōukān	Time magazine
3	阿曼达·里普利	阿曼達·里普利	Āmàndá Lǐpǔlì	Amanda Ripley
4	比尔·盖茨	比爾·蓋茨	Bǐ'ěr Gàicí	Bill Gates
5	山东	山東	Shāndōng	Shandong (province)
6	刘磊	劉磊	Liú Lěi	a person's name
7	果壳网	果殼網	Guǒké Wǎng	a science and technology website in China
8	巴图辛·米昂甘巴雅	巴圖辛·米昂甘巴雅	Bātúxīn Mǐ'ánggānbāyǎ	a person's name
9	麻省理工学院	麻省理工學院	Máshěng Lǐgōng Xuéyuàn	Massachusetts Institute of Technology
10	蒙古国	蒙古國	Ménggǔguó	Republic of Mongolia
11	伊利诺伊	伊利諾伊	Yīlìnuòyī	Illinois
12	理查德·杜尔宾	理查德·杜爾賓	Lǐchádé Dù'ěrbīn	Richard Durbin
13	希腊	希臘	Xīlà	Greece
14	艾米莉·迪金森		Àimǐlì Díjīnsēn	Emily Dickinson
15	清华大学	清華大學	Qīnghuá Dàxué	Tsinghua University
16	徐葳		Xú Wēi	a person's name
17	伯克利		Bókèlì	Berkley

| 18 | 乔治亚理工大学 | 喬治亞理工大學 | Qiáozhìyà Lǐgōng Dàxué | Georgia Institute of Technology |
| 19 | 乔治·皮特森 | 喬治·皮特森 | Qiáozhì Pítèsēn | George Peterson |

词语注释 Vocabulary and Grammar explanations

语素 (morphemes)

免-：去掉；除掉；避免；不要。(to remove; to avoid; to exempt from)

> 例 免费 免提 免票 免税 免罪 免职 免冠 免疫 免刑 免俗

-型：类型。(model; type; pattern)

> 例 新型 大型 小型 发型 线型 重型 中型 微型 流线型 巨型 造型 句型

-者：用在形容词或动词后，表示有此属性或做此动作的人或事物。
(a person who has certain attributes or does a certain activity)

> 例 提供者 学者 舞者 编者 笔者 患者 记者 作者 强者 读者 使者 长者 劳动者

首-：第一；首先。(first)

> 例 首创 首席 首演 首发 首播 首班车 首度 首推 首选 首映 首战

Lesson 4

-级：等级。(level; rank; grade)

> 例　顶级　次级　高级　低级　中级　明星级　五星级　国家级　省级　市级

增-：增加，增长。(to increase)

> 例　增长　增加　增进　增多　增高　增强

入-：进来或进去；参加。(to enter; to join)

> 例　入读　入学　入伍　入狱　入境　入手　入时　入市　入睡　入席　入选　入院

-书：1. 著作。(book)

> 例　工具书　参考书　教科书　说明书　白皮书

2. 书信；证书；文件。(letter; certificate; document)

> 例　入学通知书　悔过书　保证书　议定书　国书　婚书　家书　情书　休书　证书

重-：重新；再一次。(again; once more; re-; duplicate)

> 例　重构　重组　重建　重演　重合　重申　重围　重印　重译　重奏

-费：费用。(fee; expense; dues)

> 例　学费　饭费　伙食费　机场费　车费　旅费　路费　杂费　生活费　安家费　会员费　会费

互-： 用在单音节动词前。相互；彼此。(each other; mutual)

> 互动　互爱　互换　互敬　互让　互通　互助　互相　互谅　互利

● 四字格和成语 (four-character expressions and idioms)

● **有教无类**

这是中国古代教育家、思想家孔子提出的教育理念：不管什么人都可以受到教育，不能因为贫富、贵贱、智愚、善恶等原因把一些人排除在教育对象之外。

(This is an educational theory proposed by Confucius, an ancient Chinese philosopher. It means that in teaching we should make no class distinction and treat all students equally, regardless of their economic and social backgrounds.)

(1) 中国的思想家、教育家孔子在两千多年前提出了"**有教无类**"的教育理念。
(2) 在线教育可以使我们进一步实现"**有教无类**"的教育理念。
(3) 不论学生贫富贵贱，身为一个老师都应一视同仁、**有教无类**。
(4) 美国从小学到高中的免费教育制度是不是实现了**有教无类**的理想呢？

● **千千万万**

形容数量非常多。(thousands; many; a lot)

(1) 在现实生活中仍有**千千万万**的人由于种种原因被关在高等学府的大门之外。

(2) 中国千千万万的购房者都要面对房价不断上涨的问题。

(3) 他们一家只是千千万万中国家庭中的一个。

(4) 这首诗写得情真意切，感动了千千万万的人。

- 随时随地

任何时间、地点；时时处处；到处。(whenever and wherever possible; any time and any place; at all times and places)

(1) 这场席卷全球的"慕课教学实践"使世界上最优质的教育传播到地球最偏远的角落，也让"随时随地"的终身学习不再遥远。

(2) 有了移动网络，我可以随时随地查看电子邮件。

(3) 信用卡公司提供24小时服务，客户可以随时随地打客户热线。

(4) 这个智能手机太好了，我可以随时随地拍照。

- 与此同时

在同一时间。(at the same time; in the meantime; moreover)

(1) 我们坚信，我们可以为所有地方的所有人提供真正的顶级在线课程，不论其社会地位如何或者收入多少；与此同时，我们也力图改善学校教育质量。

(2) 欧洲央行会重新评估风险，但与此同时不会自动停止紧急流动性援助。

(3) 中国的英语教育近年来取得了很大成绩。与此同时，在这方面也还存在着一些问题。

(4) 很多非洲移民来到欧洲定居，与此同时，来自亚洲的移民也有所增加。

- **侃侃而谈**

    形容说话理直气壮、从容不迫。(to talk with confidence and composure; to talk with ease and fluency; to speak freely and frankly, sometimes boldly)

    (1) 演讲比赛中，选手们个个都是侃侃而谈，评委们不断地点头。
    (2) 王老师说话的时候，总是侃侃而谈，让人敬佩。
    (3) 他平日一向沉默寡言，想不到在辩论会上竟侃侃而谈，令人大吃一惊。
    (4) 总是侃侃而谈的人，不一定有真才实学。

- **兴趣盎然**

    形容对某种事物或某个问题兴趣浓厚的样子。(with genuine interest; with full interest)

    (1) 他每天坐在宿舍里，看着视频上的美国教授和十几个学生或侃侃而谈、或激烈争论，时不时提交自己的见解，学得兴趣盎然。
    (2) 张老师讲课总是生动有趣，使每个学生听得兴趣盎然。
    (3) 很多人在会议结束后没有离开，仍在兴趣盎然地问李教授问题，并与他合影。
    (4) 他特别喜欢网球，一谈到网球马上就兴趣盎然。

- **刮目相看**

    刮目：擦眼睛。指别人已有显著进步，不能再用老眼光看待。("刮目" literally means "to rub one's eyes"; the phrase refers to someone having made significant progress or a big advancement, so one cannot look at him/her with old eyes. Similar meanings include: "to treat somebody with increased respect; to marvel at somebody's progress and improvement".)

(1) 当时年方十五岁的巴图辛在这门课上成绩优异，让麻省理工学院刮目相看，向他发出了入学通知书。
(2) 他最近出了几本十分畅销的书，这使得很多人对他刮目相看。
(3) 另一名来自伦敦的学生说："只要我一说我在学汉语，人们就会对我刮目相看。"
(4) 小李出国留学三年归来，邻居对他都刮目相看。

● **虚词及句型** (function words and sentence patterns)

• **在于** to lie in; to rest with

动词，指出事物的本质所在，或者指出事物以什么为内容。后边要带名词、动词或分句做宾语，不能带"了""着""过"，不能带补语，不能重叠。

This is a verb that indicates where the basic truth of something lies or points out what the real content or essence of something is. It must be followed by a noun, verb, or clause as its object, and it cannot take"了"，"着"，"过"，or any complements; it also cannot be reduplicated.

(1) 在比尔·盖茨看来，发展在线教育的必要性就在于"高等教育的成本很高，人们持续学习的需求也很强烈"。
(2) 这个城市的主要问题在于污染。
(3) 一个人进步的关键在于内因。
(4) 人生的价值在于不断进取，不断进步。
(5) 问题在于没有人会相信她，所以没有人愿意帮助她。
(6) 教育的目的在于培养学生高贵的品德和人格。

- **不论 no matter**

连词，跟"无论"意义、用法相同，表示条件或者情况不同而结果不变。后面常有表示任指的疑问代词"谁""什么""怎么"等。常与"都""也""总"等副词一起用。

This is a conjunction word that is the same as "无论" in meaning and usage and indicates that a result will remain the same regardless of any conditions or situations. It is usually followed by indefinite interrogatives such as "谁"，"什么"，and "怎么"，etc. It is often used with adverbs such as "都"，"也"，"总" etc.

(1) 我们坚信，我们可以为所有地方的所有人提供真正的顶级在线课程，不论其社会地位如何或者收入多少；与此同时，我们也力图改善学校教育质量。
(2) 不论是教师或者学生，都应该遵守学校的各项规章制度。
(3) 不论你走到哪里，都别把我们这些同学忘了。
(4) 不论你问谁，都得不到答案。

- **于 (3) from; at/in**

介词，书面语，用在动词或者动宾词组之后表示处所或者来源。相当于"从""在"。

This is a preposition used in written expression after verbs or verb phrases to indicate locations or sources. It is similar to "从" or "在".

(1) 哪些人已经受益于这种新型的教育方式呢？
(2) 他之所以有机会入读美国名校，完全得益于"慕课"。
(3) 他一九八六年毕业于北京大学。
(4) 我以为他这样做是出于自愿，其实是有人指使的。

(5) 北京市空气质量的改善**得益于**改用清洁能源、限制每日出行车辆，以及更新环保型公交车和出租车等。

● **于是** then; so; thus

连词，表示后一事紧接着前一事，往往有因果关系。相当于"因此""这就""所以"等。一般用在后一分句的开始。

This is a conjunction word that indicates that one thing follows another closely, usually in a cause-effect relationship. It is similar to "因此"，"这就"，and "所以"，etc. It usually occurs at the beginning of the second clause of a complex sentence.

> 例 (1) 中国山东大学生刘磊厌倦了死板的"老师念笔记，学生记笔记"的授课方式，**于是**就在他钟爱的"果壳网"的"慕课自习室"里选修了一门Udacity的生物课，因此拥有了肤色各异的两万多名同学。
> (2) 看看离开会的时间还早，**于是**我们决定去逛书店。
> (3) 他身体不好，不能待下去了，**于是**我们便派人把他送回家去。
> (4) 眼看体弱的同学跟不上了，**于是**队长宣布休息。

● **之所以……** the reason why...; the reason for... is that...; why...

"之所以"是一个固定格式，相当于"……的原因"。后面可带动词性和形容词性词语，主要用于书面语。它用在因果复句中的第一分句指出结果，后面的分句说明原因。"之所以"常与"是因为"搭配。

This is a fixed expression similar to "……的原因". It can be followed by verbs and adjectives in written language. When it is used in a complex sentence, the first clause indicates the result or outcome, and the second clause explains the reason or cause. It is often used with "是因为".

(1) 他之所以有机会入读美国名校，完全得益于"慕课"。
(2) 之所以你现在学习成绩不好，是因为以前你没有努力学习。
(3) 我之所以错怪了你，是因为我不知道事情的起因。
(4) 我之所以有今天优秀的成绩，是与大家的热心帮助分不开的。

- 为（wéi） (1)　to be

动词，意思是"是、算作、作为、充当"。须带名词做宾语。不能带"了""着""过"，不能带补语，不能重叠，主要用于书面语。

This is a verb that means "to be, to be considered as, to act as, etc." It needs a noun to be its object. It cannot take particles "了", "着", or "过", cannot take complements, and cannot be reduplicated.

(1) 刚从美国回到清华大学的年轻学者徐葳，从伯克利大学带回了一门名为"云计算与软件工程"的在线课程。
(2) 在波士顿参加这次中文演讲比赛的学生多为大学生。
(3) 同学们都认为他成熟稳重，有组织能力，推举他为班长。
(4) 这位知名企业家最近被任命为公司的董事长。

副课文 Supplementary Text

扎克伯格清华秀中文

2014年10月22日下午，脸书的首席执行官马克·扎克伯格用出人意料的形式展示了他对中国的兴趣。他在北京清华大学的一个座谈会上用中文讲了大约半个小时。

"大家好。谢谢你们来这里。"他对听众说,"我很高兴来北京。我很爱这座城市。我的中文很糟糕,但是我每天学习中文。""我可能需要练习。"他在听众的欢笑声中补充道。他的中文远非完美,但他刚说了几个词后,在场的学生和老师就报以热烈的掌声和欢呼声。

当被问到为什么学中文时,扎克伯格解释道:"第一,我太太是中国人。她在家说中文,她的奶奶只说中文。我想要跟她们说话。当我用中文告诉她奶奶我们要结婚时,她的奶奶非常吃惊。第二,中国是伟大的国家,所以我想学中文。第三,普通话很难,我一直说英文,但我喜欢挑战。"

此次到访清华,扎克伯格是以清华经管顾问委员会委员的身份来参加会议的。他说:"我非常关心教育,我在美国做了很多支持教育的事情。我希望参加清华经管委员会,了解和支持中国的教育。"在和清华大学校长陈吉宁的交谈中,扎克伯格结合他的个人职业经历,分享了他对于人才培养的看法。他表示,大学应培养具有扎实的知识和较强的组织管理能力及领导力的创新人才。

扎克伯格访问北京坚持用中文与学生交流这一消息在中国和美国网民中引起了巨大反响。在中国,有人称赞他说:"他能成功与他的才华、智慧和毅力分不开!很多老外觉得中文很难,而他做到了!"也有人则被他的苦心感动了:"看了一段还是蛮感慨的,他应该比这个世界上99%的人都忙,依然还挤时间学习一门新的语言,而且还敢于在公开的场合使用,说明他的成功不是偶然的。"

微软创始人比尔·盖茨在2015年1月28日参加美国社交新闻社区的《有问必答》节目时表示:他对扎克伯格能够说中文表示惊讶和羡慕。他说:"扎克伯格竟然学会了普通话并且能对中国学生提的问题进行回答——这简直难以置信。""我觉得我很笨,我不会说外语。我在高中的时候曾经上过拉丁文和希腊文课,帮助我扩大了词汇量,但是我更期望我能够掌握法语、阿拉伯语或者中文。"讲一口流利中文的澳大利亚前总理陆克文也非常认同扎克伯格的表现,在署名"老陆"的微博上,他写到:

"更多的西方人应该向马克学习,来学中文,来了解中国,因为中国的未来是我们共同的未来。"

讨论题 Discussion

根据课文内容回答下列问题
(Please answer the following questions based on the text)

1. 扎克伯格为什么学习中文?他与你学习中文的目的一样吗?
2. 扎克伯格为什么来到清华大学?他对人才培养有什么看法?
3. 中国人对扎克伯格用中文谈话交流有什么反响?
4. 比尔·盖茨对扎克伯格说中文怎么看?他有什么样的外语学习经历?
5. 陆克文是谁?他为什么支持和鼓励西方人学中文?

生词 New Words

1	出人意料		chūrén-yìliào	f.e.	to exceed all expectations, surprising
2	座谈会	座談會	zuòtánhuì	n.	conference, symposium
3	听众	聽眾	tīngzhòng	n.	audience, listeners
4	欢笑	歡笑	huānxiào	v.	to laugh heartily
5	完美		wánměi	adj.	perfect, flawless
6	掌声	掌聲	zhǎngshēng	n.	clapping, applause
7	欢呼	歡呼	huānhū	v.	to cheer, to hail
8	普通话	普通話	pǔtōnghuà	n.	Mandarin Chinese
9	到访	到訪	dàofǎng	v.	to come for a visit

10	经管	經管	jīngguǎn	n.	economics and management
11	顾问	顧問	gùwèn	n.	adviser, consultant
12	委员会	委員會	wěiyuánhuì	n.	committee, council
13	交谈	交談	jiāotán	v.	to talk, to converse, to chat
14	扎实	扎實	zhāshi	adj.	solid, sound, strong
15	网民	網民	wǎngmín	n.	internet user
16	反响	反響	fǎnxiǎng	n.	reaction, echo, repercussion
17	才华	才華	cáihuá	n.	talent, gifts, literary or artistic talent
18	智慧		zhìhuì	n.	wisdom, intelligence, wit
19	毅力		yìlì	n.	willpower, tenacity, perseverance
20	老外		lǎowài	n.	foreigner (colloquial expression)
21	苦心		kǔxīn	n.	trouble taken, painstaking efforts
22	蛮	蠻	mán	b.f./ adv.	quite, pretty, very
23	敢于	敢於	gǎnyú	v.	to dare to, to have the courage to
24	场合	場合	chǎnghé	n.	occasion, situation, conjuncture
25	偶然		ǒurán	adj.	accidental, fortuitous, occasional
26	创始人	創始人	chuàngshǐrén	n.	founder, originator, creator
27	有问必答	有問必答	yǒuwèn-bìdá	f.e.	to answer every question
28	竟然		jìngrán	adv.	unexpectedly, to one's surprise
29	简直	簡直	jiǎnzhí	adv.	simply, at all
30	难以置信	難以置信	nányǐzhìxìn	f.e.	unbelievable, incredible
31	高中		gāozhōng	n.	high school
32	拉丁文		Lādīngwén	n.	Latin
33	希腊文	希臘文	Xīlàwén	n.	Greek

34	词汇	詞彙	cíhuì	n.	vocabulary, lexicon, glossary
35	阿拉伯语	阿拉伯語	Ālābóyǔ	n.	Arabic
36	署名		shǔ míng	v.o.	to sign (a signature)
37	微博		wēibó	n.	microblog or tweets

专有名词 Proper nouns

1	马克·扎克伯格	馬克·扎克伯格	Mǎkè Zhākèbógé	Mark Zuckerberg
2	清华	清華	Qīnghuá	Tsinghua University, China
3	脸书	臉書	Liǎnshū	Facebook
4	陈吉宁	陳吉寧	Chén Jíníng	*a person's name*
5	微软	微軟	Wēiruǎn	Microsoft
6	陆克文	陸克文	Lù Kèwén	Kevin Rudd

奥运会与兴奋剂

第 5 课

主课文 Main Text

随着1896年现代奥林匹克运动的兴起，兴奋剂就成为与之共生的"肿瘤"。参加奥运比赛的选手使用兴奋剂的历史可以说是"源远流长"。现代奥运史上最早的服用兴奋剂的事件发生在1904年的美国圣路易斯第三届现代奥林匹克运动会上。当年的马拉松比赛冠军是美籍英国人托马斯·希克斯。在比赛过程中，他的教练一直拿着注射器跟随着他。当希克斯精疲力竭之时，教练给他注射了一针"士的宁"，并给他喝下一大杯威士忌。这些都能帮助他增强体能或控制能力，提高比赛成绩。在体育比赛中服用兴奋剂，在近代和现代更为流行。自20世纪60年代初以来，国际奥林匹克委员会就一直坚持不懈地反对服用兴奋剂。可是，在2012年伦敦奥运会上又出现了12例兴奋剂丑闻。奥运会与兴奋剂在进行的是一场没有硝烟的战争，并且似乎看不到尽头。

奥运会的目的是通过体育运动增进各国的相互了解和友谊，从而建立一个更加美好的和平世界。但一些运动员却忘记了公平竞争的原则，为了得到更多的奖牌和奖金，服用了兴奋剂，结果却往往是被取消了所获得的奖牌和比赛的资格。另外，兴奋剂虽然能提高运动员的比赛成绩，但是会对他们的身体造成极大的伤害。这样的例子在奥运会的历史上举不胜举。1960年，丹麦自行车选手延森在罗马奥运会比赛中死亡，尸检证明他服用了苯丙胺、酒精和另一种扩张血管的药物；1967年，英国自行车运动员辛普森死于环法比赛途中，死时衣袋中还有未吃完的苯丙胺；1988年汉城奥运会后，田径运动员本·约翰逊因被查出使用了兴奋剂而被剥夺成绩并禁赛两年。他的两次世界纪录也被随之取消。2000年12月27日，马利昂·琼斯在悉尼奥运会上获得了五枚奖牌，被称为"女飞人"。但是，当查出她是靠服兴奋剂取得好成绩后，她被称为"体坛骗子"。2013年美国著名运动员阿姆斯特朗称自己使用违禁药物，国际自行车联盟正式宣布了对他的处罚，包括终身禁赛、剥夺七个环法自行车赛冠军头衔。2014年1月，两位韩国男羽毛球运动员因为违反了羽联反兴奋剂条例，被处以禁赛一年的重罚。

在动画片《猫和老鼠》中，猫想抓住老鼠，和老鼠斗智斗勇。反兴奋剂和兴奋剂之间的斗争也像是猫捉老鼠。随着医学的发展，兴奋剂不断更新变化，越来越难以检测。在与兴奋剂这只"老鼠"的追逐中，反兴奋剂这只"猫"始终在追赶。为此，国际奥委会规定，参加奥运会选手的尿样或者是血样将在实验室存放八年。在这段时间里，专家们将进行各种化验来检测选手们是否服用了此前查不出来的违禁药物。

随着体育商业化的不断深入，参与体育运动所获得的利益也不断提高。在利益的驱使下，一些运动员不惜牺牲自己的前途和健康服用兴奋剂。2008年一项调查显示，在澳大利亚，几乎有三分之一的运动员表示会考虑使用兴奋剂提高成绩。由此看来，只要体育仍旧与荣耀、金钱相连，这场兴奋剂和反兴奋剂之间的斗争，就一天不会终止。

Lesson 5
奥运会与兴奋剂

讨论题 Discussion

根据课文内容回答下列问题
(Please answer the following questions based on the text)

1. 为什么说兴奋剂是与奥运会共生的"肿瘤"？
2. 我们为什么要反兴奋剂？
3. 你觉得那些使用兴奋剂的人该不该受到处罚？该受什么样的处罚？
4. 为什么说反兴奋剂和兴奋剂之间的斗争就像是猫捉老鼠？
5. 你觉得运动员最终会完全停止使用兴奋剂吗？为什么？

生词 New Words

1	兴奋剂	興奮劑	xīngfènjì	n.	stimulant, dope, performance enhancement drugs
2	共生		gòngshēng	v.	to grow together; intergrowth, to paragenesis, symbiosis
3	肿瘤	腫瘤	zhǒngliú	n.	tumor
4	选手	選手	xuǎnshǒu	n.	athlete selected for a sports meet, player, contestant
5	史		shǐ	b.f./n.	history
6	服用		fúyòng	v.	to take (medicine)
7	马拉松	馬拉松	mǎlāsōng	n.	marathon
8	教练	教練	jiàoliàn	n.	coach
9	注射		zhùshè	v.	to inject
10	器		qì	b.f.	instrument, apparatus, weapon
11	跟随	跟隨	gēnsuí	v.	to follow, to go after

12	精疲力竭		jīngpí-lìjié	adj.	worn out, exhausted
13	威士忌		wēishìjì	n.	whisky, whiskey
14	体能	體能	tǐnéng	n.	stamina, physical ability, fitness
15	近代		jìndài	n.	modern times
16	不懈		búxiè	adj.	untiring, unremitting, indefatigable
17	丑闻	醜聞	chǒuwén	n.	scandal
18	尽头	盡頭	jìntóu	n.	end, extremity
19	增进	增進	zēngjìn	v.	to enhance, to promote
20	各国	各國	gèguó	n.	each country, every country
21	公平		gōngpíng	adj.	fair, just, impartial
22	奖牌	獎牌	jiǎngpái	n.	medal
23	奖金	獎金	jiǎngjīn	n.	bonus, prize, premium
24	资格	資格	zīgé	n.	qualifications
25	尸检	屍檢	shījiǎn	v.	autopsy
26	酒精		jiǔjīng	n.	alcohol, spirit, ethyl alcohol
27	血管		xuèguǎn	n.	blood vessel, vein, artery
28	药物	藥物	yàowù	n.	medicines, drugs, pharmaceuticals
29	途		tú	b.f.	way, path, route
30	衣袋		yīdài	n.	pocket
31	田径运动员	田徑運動員	tiánjìng yùndòngyuán	n.p.	track and field athletes
32	剥夺	剝奪	bōduó	v.	to deprive, to expropriate, to strip (of)
33	禁赛	禁賽	jìnsài	v.	suspend, to ban (from a specific sports)
34	纪录	紀錄	jìlù	n.	record
35	枚		méi	m(n)	measure word for coins, needle, small objects

36	飞人	飛人	fēirén	n.	flying man, fast runner
37	体坛	體壇	tǐtán	n.	sports circles, the sporting world
38	骗子	騙子	piànzi	n.	cheater, liar, swindler
39	违禁	違禁	wéijìn	attr./v.	banned, prohibited; to violate a ban
40	联盟	聯盟	liánméng	n.	league, union, coalition
41	头衔	頭銜	tóuxián	n.	official title, academic rank or title
42	条例	條例	tiáolì	n.	regulations, rules, ordinances
43	罚	罰	fá	v.	to punish, to penalize, to discipline
44	动画片	動畫片	dònghuàpiàn	n.	animated cartoon, animated film
45	抓住		zhuāzhù	v(c)	to capture, to catch hold of
46	斗	鬥	dòu	v.	to fight, to tussle
47	智		zhì	b.f./n.	wisdom, intelligence, brainpower
48	勇		yǒng	b.f./n.	courage, bravery
49	更新		gēngxīn	v.	to renew, to replace, to update
50	检测	檢測	jiǎncè	v.	to check, to test, to examine
51	追逐		zhuīzhú	v.	to pursue, to chase
52	追赶	追趕	zhuīgǎn	v.	to chase after, to pursue
53	尿		niào	n./v.	urine; to urinate
54	血样	血樣	xuèyàng	n.	blood samples
55	实验室	實驗室	shíyànshì	n.	laboratory
56	存放		cúnfàng	v.	to store, to leave with
57	化验	化驗	huàyàn	v.	to do laboratory test
58	此前		cǐqián	n.	prior to a given time or event
59	驱使	驅使	qūshǐ	v.	to drive, to propel, to prompt

60	不惜		bùxī	v.	not stint, not spare, at all costs
61	仍旧	仍舊	réngjiù	adv.	still, yet
62	荣耀	榮耀	róngyào	n.	honor, glory
63	相连	相連	xiānglián	v.	to link, to connect
64	终止	終止	zhōngzhǐ	v.	to stop, to end

专有名词 Proper nouns

1	奥林匹克	奥林匹克	Àolínpǐkè	Olympics
2	奥运	奧運	Àoyùn	the Olympics
3	圣路易斯	聖路易斯	Shènglùyìsī	Saint Louis, a city in Missouri, U.S.A
4	托马斯·希克斯	托馬斯·希克斯	Tuōmǎsī Xīkèsī	Thomas Hicks
5	士的宁	士的寧	Shìdìníng	strychnine
6	奥林匹克委员会	奥林匹克委員會	Àolínpǐkè Wěiyuánhuì	Olympic Committee
7	延森		Yánsēn	Jensen
8	罗马	羅馬	Luómǎ	Rome
9	苯丙胺		Běnbǐng'àn	amphetamine
10	辛普森		Xīnpǔsēn	Simpsons
11	汉城	漢城	Hànchéng	Seoul, capital of the Republic of Korea
12	本·约翰逊	本·約翰遜	Běn Yuēhànxùn	Ben Johnson
13	马利昂·琼斯	馬利昂·瓊斯	Mǎlì'áng Qióngsī	Marion Jones
14	悉尼		Xīní	Sydney, Australia
15	阿姆斯特朗		Āmǔsītèlǎng	Lance Armstrong
16	韩国	韓國	Hánguó	Republic of Korea

| 17 | 羽联 | 羽聯 | Yǔlián | Badminton World Federation |
| 18 | 奥委会 | 奧委會 | Àowěihuì | the abbreviation for Olympic Committee |

词语注释 Vocabulary and Grammar explanations

语素 (morphemes)

-剂： 制剂。(pharmaceutical or other chemical solvent)

> 例　兴奋剂　杀虫剂　润滑剂　洗洁剂　洗发剂　灭火剂

-器： 泛指用具。(utensil; apparatus)

> 例　注射器　武器　木器　银器　金器　瓷器　消音器　灭火器

-物： 物件，东西。(article; thing)

> 例　药物　衣物　遗物　食物　读物　财物　动物　废物　怪物

-牌： 用木板、金属片或其他材料做成的标志。(plate; sign; tablet)

> 例　奖牌　广告牌　门牌　路牌　指示牌　木牌

-坛： 指文艺、体育等某一领域。(the areas of literature, art, or sports)

> 例　文坛　体坛　影坛　诗坛　乒坛　舞坛　政坛

-手： 专司某事或擅长某种技艺的人。(a person good at certain things or doing a certain job)

> 例　选手　杀手　水手　舵手　助手　棋手　旗手　骑手　射手　歌手

四字格和成语 (four-character expressions and idioms)

● **源远流长**

指传统或历史长久。(This means "to have a long history".)

(1) 参加奥运比赛的选手使用兴奋剂的历史可以说是"源远流长"。
(2) 中国和韩国互为近邻，文化相近，人民相亲，人文交流源远流长。
(3) 中华饮食文化源远流长，各地的饮食也自成特色。
(4) 端午节包粽子、赛龙舟是源远流长的文化习俗，至今仍在民间广泛流行。

● **精疲力竭**

精神和身体极度疲劳。(This means, literally, "spirit weary, strength exhausted".)

(1) 当希克斯精疲力竭之时，教练给他注射了一针"士的宁"，并给他喝下一大杯威士忌。
(2) 上班族完成一天的工作后，常常是精疲力竭。
(3) 比赛后，他精疲力竭地躺在地上起不来。
(4) 负伤的狮子逃亡四十个小时，最后精疲力竭，被猎人打死了。

● **坚持不懈**

懈：松懈。做事持之以恒，坚持到底，一点儿不松懈。("懈" means "slack"; this expression means "to persevere unremittingly, without being lax even a bit".)

(1) 国际奥林匹克委员会就一直坚持不懈地反对服用兴奋剂。

(2) 前新加坡领导人李光耀也曾坚持不懈地学习汉语，直到 90 高龄还保持着学习汉语的习惯。
(3) 中国长期以来一直坚持不懈地帮助非洲人民。
(4) 想要有健康的身体，健康的饮食和坚持不懈的运动缺一不可。

- **斗智斗勇**

斗：争斗；智：智慧，聪明；勇：勇气，勇力。用智谋和勇力来争胜负，指竞争。（"斗" means "to fight"；"智" means "wits"；"勇" means "courage". This expression overall means "to fight using wit and courage".）

 (1) 在动画片《猫和老鼠》中，猫想抓住老鼠，和老鼠斗智斗勇。
(2) 商场的竞争也需要勇气和智慧，所以商战也常常要斗智斗勇。
(3) 《三国志演义》是一部有名的中国历史小说，里面充满了政治和军事上的斗智斗勇。
(4) 她在电视剧和电影中常常扮演间谍的角色，跟敌人斗智斗勇。

● **虚词及句型** (function words and sentence patterns)

- **为（wéi）(2)**

动词，类似后缀。某些单音节副词、形容词带上"为"字共同修饰双音节形容词、动词，比如说，甚为、更为、极为、大为、深为、颇为、广为。一般用于书面语。

This is a verb that is used as a suffix. Some monosyllable adverb and adjective words combine with "为" to modify disyllable adjectives and verbs, for example: "甚为，更为，极为，大为，深为，颇为，广为"; usually "为" is used in written expression.

(1) 在体育比赛中服用兴奋剂在近代和现代更为流行。
(2) 爱因斯坦和乔布斯在科学界的地位极为重要。
(3) Lady gaga的歌在世界上广为流传。
(4) 市民对政府的新政策颇为不满。

● **因……而……** because of..., somebody/something

固定搭配，表示因果关系。"因"后面跟着的部分说明原因，"而"后面的部分说明结果或者后果。

This is a fixed usage, indicating a cause-effect relationship. What follows "因" is the reason or cause; what follows "而" is the effect or consequence.

(1) 田径运动员本·约翰逊因被查出使用了兴奋剂而被剥夺成绩并禁赛两年。
(2) 她因健康状况不佳而被迫放弃了工作。
(3) 他因跟同事不和而离开了公司。
(4) 杭州和苏州因风景优美而闻名世界。

● **随之** following...; as a result...

固定用法。"之"在此指代前面分句中提到的事物或者情况。"随之"用在第二个分句中说明后面的情况随着前面而产生或发生变化。

This is a fixed expression, where "之" refers to what is mentioned in the first clause. "随之" appears in the second clause to indicate a change has taken place, or a consequence has occurred due to what happened in the first clause.

(1) 本·约翰逊因被查出使用了兴奋剂而被剥夺成绩并禁赛两年。他的两次世界纪录也被随之取消。
(2) 炒股能赚钱，但高风险也随之而来。
(3) 大城市的房价越来越高，大学毕业生的压力也随之越来越重。
(4) 互联网的发展给人们的生活带来了很多方便，但是其负面影响也随之出现。

● 以

介词。"单音节动词＋以"有"给与"的意思，比如说，处以、致以、用以、授以等。用于书面表达。

This is a preposition. A monosyllable "verb + 以" indicates "to give or grant", for example: "处以，致以，用以，授以，etc." This is a written expression.

(1) 2014年1月，两位韩国男羽毛球运动员因为违反了羽联反兴奋剂条例，被处以禁赛一年的重罚。
(2) 他向在战争中牺牲的士兵致以崇高的敬意。
(3) 政府将一部分资金用以改善城市公共交通。
(4) 他被授以博士学位。

● 只要……就……　so long as... (then)...

连词，表示必要条件。"只要"可用在主语前或后，"只要"后边的条件不是唯一的条件。

This is a conjunction that indicates a required condition. "只要" can be used before or after the subject. The condition following "只要" is not the only condition.

(1) 由此看来，只要体育仍旧与荣耀、金钱相连，这场兴奋剂和反兴奋剂之间的斗争，就一天不会终止。

(2) 每个星期你只要运动两天，就能保持身体健康。

(3) 广告说："只要一美元，你就能买到喜欢的比萨。"

(4) 在一些大城市，由于排水系统不太好，只要一下暴雨，在街上就能"看海"。

副课文 Supplementary Text

现代人和慢运动

现代人爱把"放空"二字挂在嘴边。总想暂时放开工作和生活的烦恼，好好休息一阵子，让心灵沉淀。但现实又总是让"放空"的愿望显得奢侈。放慢生活，是想在生活中找到平衡。运动同样如此。德国科学家说，运动的真正目标不是为了更疲惫，而是更健康。

慢运动指的是一些强度较小、节奏较慢、适宜长期练习的休闲体育项目，比如瑜伽、太极拳、射箭、棋牌、散步等。上海交通大学教授赵文杰告诉记者，现代人普遍工作压力大、生活节奏快，对运动的态度有两种：要么不运动，要么拼命运动。他们平时缺乏规律性锻炼，强度太大的运动容易造成运动损伤。慢运动既是一种方式，也是一种理念。慢运动还可以跟生活相结合，比如说园艺、木工，都是一种运动。时下，很多年轻人喜欢射箭、钓鱼等休闲体育活动。工作中可能表现得风风火火，但选择的运动却需要静心和耐心，这也是一种通过运动改善性格的途径。对于那些处事不够冷静沉着，易冲动急躁的人来说，静态的慢运动不会带来情绪的波动，有助于增强自我控制能力。

早在上世纪80年代，著名企业家马云就痴迷于打太极拳和下围棋。从

第 6 课

道德还是自由：
美国堕胎合法化之争

主课文 Main Text

堕胎到底是违背道德准则还是维护自由权利？这是美国人永恒的话题。一般而言，民主党和持自由主义观点的人认同堕胎行为的合理性；而共和党和保守主义者则认为，堕胎行为无异于谋杀，是不道德的。来自南方保守势力大本营的布什在任内推动了禁止晚期堕胎的立法，但民主党人奥巴马一上台，就开始清算布什的政策。近年来，围绕堕胎合法化的争论愈演愈烈。

南达科他州州长签署禁止堕胎的法令

南达科他州州长迈克·朗兹 2006 年 3 月 6 日签署了一项禁止堕胎的法案。这项法律禁止州内几乎所有的堕胎行为，甚至包括受害人被强奸或乱伦而导致的怀孕。唯一的例外是孕妇的生命受到了威胁，否则，实施堕胎手术的医生就被视为违法，最高可判处五年监禁。身为共和党人的朗兹州长在签署法案后发表了一份书面声明称："在世界历史上，对于文明的真正考验是看人们怎样对待社会上最弱势和无助的群体。这项法案的发起者和支持者们相信，堕胎是错误的，因为未出世的孩子是我们社会中最弱势也是最无助的人。我认同他们的意见。"这项法案与1973年美国联邦最高法院认定堕胎合法的"罗诉韦德案"划时代判决背道而驰。经营南达科他州唯一堕胎诊所的"家庭计划联盟"称，这项法律"悍然违宪"，极其危险，而且得不到大多数美国人的支持。该组织表示，他们将采取一切必要手段——不管是提起联邦诉讼或是发动南达科他州全民公投，来废止这项法律。

医生乔治·蒂勒遭人枪杀

2009年5月31日，因提供晚期堕胎而颇具争议性的美国医生乔治·蒂勒在堪萨斯州堪萨斯城遭人枪杀。蒂勒当年67岁，他不仅坚持做堕胎手术，还为怀孕20周以上的孕妇做晚期堕胎手术，是美国少数几个坚持做晚期堕胎手术的医生之一。正因如此，蒂勒一直是反堕胎人士的主要攻击目标之一。他的诊所门前经常有反堕胎组织举行大规模抗议活动，一些反堕胎者也常常在他居住的社区发放传单。此前，蒂勒已遭到数次攻击。枪杀事件发生后，美国反堕胎组织也发表声明对枪杀行为表示谴责，称他们希望用合法的手段来击倒蒂勒。奥巴马总统对该事件感到震惊及愤怒，他的声明写道："无论美国人在像堕胎这样的富有争议的问题上分歧有多大，都不应该用暴力这样恶劣的行动来解决争端。"

1973年的"罗诉韦德案"

对美国而言，堕胎到底应不应该合法化一直是各州争论不休的论题。最近一项民调显示，过半数的美国人都认为应该将堕胎合法化，但同样有过半数者认为这是道德犯罪。1973年的"罗诉韦德案"跟60年代发生的两件事有密切关系，使得人们更加倾向于将堕胎合法化。

1962年，一个叫谢里·芬克拜的妇女，发现自己怀孕两个月了，但她曾不慎服用过会导致胎儿畸形的镇静药，于是她寻求堕胎，并取得了医院审查委员会的同意。然而消息公布后，州检察官扬言要将她逮捕，于是医生不得不放弃了手术。谢里·芬克拜不得不专程前往瑞典做手术。此一事件将堕胎问题的辩论推进到一个新的层面：如果剥夺胎儿的生存权利是不道德的，那么我们应不应该为了坚守这种道德意识，而将明明有问题的胎儿也生下来？

另一件事则是，1966年旧金山流行麻疹，很多人都被感染了。这种麻疹的并发症有可能导致孕妇死亡以及胎儿的先天性畸形。于是当地的21名医生不顾禁令，为感染麻疹的孕妇做了堕胎手术，结果遭到逮捕。此事经新闻报道后，引发了更多人对禁止堕胎的不满。

终于，在1973年1月22日联邦最高法院对"罗诉韦德案"的判决中，将堕胎合法化。

讨论题 Discussion

根据课文内容回答下列问题

(Please answer the following questions based on the text)

1. 对待堕胎问题，美国的民主党和共和党的观点有什么不同？
2. 支持堕胎和反对堕胎的各方各自的理由是什么？
3. 你支持堕胎还是反对堕胎？为什么？
4. 如果一个妇女由于被强奸而导致怀孕或者由于用药导致胎儿畸形，那么这个妇女有没有权利堕胎？为什么？
5. 1973年的"罗诉韦德案"最终判决是什么？这个判决跟两个什么样的事件有关系？

生词 New Words

#					
1	堕胎	墮胎	duò tāi	v.o.	abortion; to abort
2	永恒		yǒnghéng	adj.	eternal, perpetual
3	自由主义	自由主義	zìyóu zhǔyì	n.p.	liberalism
4	主义	主義	zhǔyì	n.	systematic doctrine or theory, -ism
5	无异	無異	wúyì	v.	to be not different from
6	大本营	大本營	dàběnyíng	n.	headquarter, base camp
7	晚期		wǎnqī	n.	later period, late stage
8	上台	上臺	shàng tái	v.o.	to appear on the stage, to come (or rise) to power, to assume power
9	清算		qīngsuàn	v.	to carefully calculate and check, to expose and criticize all evil-doings or mistakes, and inflict punishment
10	愈演愈烈		yùyǎn-yùliè	f.e.	to grow in intensity, to intensify
11	州长	州長	zhōuzhǎng	n.	governor
12	签署	簽署	qiānshǔ	v.	to sign officially, to subscribe
13	强奸	強姦	qiángjiān	v.	to rape, to assault sexually
14	乱伦	亂倫	luànlún	v.	to be incestuous, to commit incest
15	怀孕	懷孕	huái yùn	v.o.	to be pregnant, to conceive
16	孕妇	孕婦	yùnfù	n.	pregnant woman, gravida
17	视	視	shì	b.f.	to look at, to regard
18	违法	違法	wéi fǎ	v.o.	to break the law, to be illegal
19	判处	判處	pànchǔ	v.	to sentence, to condemn, to penalize
20	监禁	監禁	jiānjìn	v.	to take into custody, to imprison

Lesson 6

道德还是自由：美国堕胎合法化之争

21	书面	書面	shūmiàn	n.	written, in written form, in writing
22	考验	考驗	kǎoyàn	n./v.	test, trial; to put sb. to the test
23	弱势	弱勢	ruòshì	adj.	weak, vulnerable
24	无助	無助	wúzhù	adj.	helpless
25	发起	發起	fāqǐ	v.	to initiate, to start, to launch
26	出世		chūshì	v.	to be born, to come into the world
27	认定	認定	rèndìng	v.	firmly believe, to affirm
28	划时代	劃時代	huàshídài	adj.	epoch making
29	背道而驰	背道而馳	bèidào-érchí	f.e	to go in the opposite direction
30	诊所	診所	zhěnsuǒ	n.	clinic
31	悍然		hànrán	adv.	outrageously, brazenly, flagrantly
32	违	違	wéi	b.f.	to disobey, to violate
33	宪	憲	xiàn	b.f.	constitution, law, statute
34	或是		huòshì	conj.	or, perhaps
35	全民		quánmín	n.	nation-wide, all the people, the entire people
36	公投		gōngtóu	n.	referendum
37	废止	廢止	fèizhǐ	v.	to abolish, to annul, to put an end to
38	颇	頗	pō	adv.	quite, very, considerably
39	抗议	抗議	kàngyì	v.	to protest
40	居住		jūzhù	v.	to live, to reside, to dwell
41	发放	發放	fāfàng	v.	to send out, to give out, to provide
42	传单	傳單	chuándān	n.	leaflet, handbill, flyer
43	谴责	譴責	qiǎnzé	v.	to condemn, to denounce, to criticize

44	富有		fùyǒu	v./adj.	to be full of ; wealthy, rich
45	恶劣	惡劣	èliè	adj.	bad, despicable, nasty
46	争端	爭端	zhēngduān	n.	dispute, controversy, conflict
47	不休		bùxiū	adv.	endlessly, ceaselessly
48	论题	論題	lùntí	n.	topic
49	民调	民調	míndiào	n.	opinion poll
50	合法化		héfǎhuà	v.	to legalize, to make legal
51	慎		shèn	b.f./n.	careful, cautious
52	胎儿	胎兒	tāi'ér	n.	fetus, embryo
53	镇静	鎮靜	zhènjìng	adj.	sedative, calm, composed
54	审查	審查	shěnchá	v.	to examine, to inspect, to investigate
55	检察官	檢察官	jiǎncháguān	n.	public prosecutor
56	扬言	揚言	yáng yán	v.o.	to threaten
57	逮捕		dàibǔ	v.	to arrest
58	专程	專程	zhuānchéng	adv.	special trip
59	前往		qiánwǎng	v.	to go, to leave for, to proceed to
60	推进	推進	tuījìn	v.	to advance, to push on, to carry forward
61	坚守	堅守	jiānshǒu	v.	to stick to, to hold fast to, to stand fast
62	明明		míngmíng	adv.	obviously, plainly, undoubtedly
63	麻疹	痲疹	mázhěn	n.	measles, rubeola
64	并发症	併發症	bìngfāzhèng	n.	complication
65	不顾	不顧	búgù	v.	to disregard, to ignore
66	不满	不滿	bùmǎn	adj.	resentful, discontented, dissatisfied

Lesson 6 第6课 道德还是自由: 美国堕胎合法化之争

专有名词 Proper nouns

1	南达科他	南達科他	Nándákētā	South Dokota
2	迈克·朗兹	邁克·朗茲	Màikè Lǎngzī	Mike Rounds
3	罗诉韦德案	羅訴韋德案	Luó Sù Wéidé Àn	Roe versus Wade Case
4	乔治·蒂勒	喬治·蒂勒	Qiáozhì Dìlè	George Taylor
5	堪萨斯州	堪薩斯州	Kānsàsī Zhōu	Kansas
6	堪萨斯城	堪薩斯城	Kānsàsī Chéng	Kansas City
7	谢里·芬克拜	謝里·芬克拜	Xièlǐ Fēnkèbài	Sherri Finkbine
8	瑞典		Ruìdiǎn	Sweden

词语注释 Vocabulary and Grammar Explanations

● 语素 (morphemes)

-期: 一段时间。 (a period of time; phase; stage)

> 例 晚期 早期 中期 更年期 假期 暑期 婚期 工期 预产期
> 学期 花期 青春期 汛期 前期 后期

-人: 指某种人。 (person; person who is engaged in a particular activity)

> 例 受害人 捐款人 收信人 证婚人 辩护人 奠基人 过来人
> 买卖人 代理人 文化人 自己人 同路人 陌生人 读书人
> 创始人 候选人 代言人 发言人

91

反-: 反抗，反对。(to oppose; anti-; counter-)

> 例 反堕胎　反战　反革命　反作用　反政府　反社会　反传统
>   反潮流　反导弹　反科学　反作用

-形: 形状。(shape)

> 例 畸形　圆形　方形　地形　三角形　圆锥形　队形　波形　体形
>   条形　图形　字形　象形　外形

-药: 药物。(medicine)

> 例 镇静药　胃药　毒药　补药　中药　西药　草药　良药　头疼药
>   止痛药

● 四字格和成语 (four-character expressions and idioms)

● 愈演愈烈

事情或情况变得越来越严重。(getting worse or becoming increasingly fierce; to intensify)

> 例 (1) 近年来，围绕堕胎合法化的争论愈演愈烈。
> (2) 自从去年10月份以来，暴力活动就有愈演愈烈之势。
> (3) 在中国迈向市场经济的今天，企业间的竞争愈演愈烈。
> (4) 虽然大家都知道进入名校不一定保证孩子将来的成功，可是家长们追求名校之风还是愈演愈烈。

● 背道而驰

朝着相反的方向走。比喻彼此的做法、目的完全相反。(to run in opposite directions; to draw further apart; to be opposed to)

（1）这项法案与1973年美国联邦最高法院认定堕胎合法的"罗诉韦德案"划时代判决背道而驰。
（2）他现在的一言一行已经与自己以前的做人原则背道而驰。
（3）如果你的设想和你想要达到的目标背道而驰，那么你必须改变它。
（4）不这么做的话，等于是与美国人所坚持的一切背道而驰。

虚词及句型 (function words and sentence patterns)

无异于 not different from

动词，没有什么不同，用于书面语。

This is a verb meaning "to be not different from" and is used in written language.

（1）共和党和保守主义者认为，堕胎行为无异于谋杀，是不道德的。
（2）这项贷款对于贫困家庭及其子女来说无异于一个福音，孩子上大学有了希望。
（3）当今时代，信息无所不在，但要从中查找特定信息，是件非常费时的事，无异于大海捞针。
（4）他向不懂音乐的人讲解其妙处，无异于对牛弹琴。

而 then, so, thus, therefore

连词，连接事理上前后相因的成分，表示因果、目的等关系。

This is a conjunction word, used for cause-effect relationships or a purpose or goal.

（1）这项法律禁止州内几乎所有的堕胎行为，甚至包括受害人被强奸或乱伦而导致的怀孕。

(2) 那朵花由于缺水而死了，很可惜。

(3) 他由于表现出色而得到提升，工资也随之大涨。

(4) 她为了学好汉语而来到中国。

- **否则** otherwise

连词，表示"如果不是这样"，连接分句，用在后一个分句的前面。用于书面语。

This is a conjunction word, meaning "if it is not so". It is used at the beginning of the second clause in a complex sentence. It is a written expression.

(1) 这项法律禁止州内几乎所有的堕胎行为，甚至包括受害人被强奸或乱伦而导致的怀孕。唯一的例外是孕妇的生命受到了威胁。否则，实施堕胎手术的医生就被视为违法，最高可判处五年监禁。

(2) 有异议的请现在提出，否则请保持沉默。

(3) 大概是有什么重要的事，否则他不会连续打电话给你。

(4) 你必须在四月完成论文，否则很难在今年六月毕业。

- **被视为** to be considered as

固定搭配，表示被动，意思是"被看成""被看作"。后面须带宾语。"被"和"视为"可以分开。

This is a fixed expression indicating passive voice and means "to be considered as". It should be followed by an object, and "被" and "视为" can be separated in a sentence.

(1) 这项法律禁止州内几乎所有的堕胎行为，甚至包括受害人被强奸或乱伦而导致的怀孕。唯一的例外是孕妇的生命受到了威胁。否则，实施堕胎手术的医生就**被视为**违法，最高可判处五年监禁。
(2) 她**被视为**中国最具国际影响力的女演员。
(3) 对一个印第安人直呼其名，或直接问她的名字，都**被视为**无礼的行为。
(4) 男女平等，**被**当今社会**视为**天经地义，那可是经过长期努力才有的结果。

• 对……而言　regarding; with regard to; as far as

固定搭配，相当于"对……来说"，把要谈论的对象单独提出来并加以强调。

This is a fixed expression, similar to "对……来说" in meaning, and is used to emphasize the topic that will be discussed in the sentence.

(1) **对**美国**而言**，堕胎到底应不应该合法化一直是各州争议不休的论题。
(2) **对**我**而言**，这个问题一点儿都不难解决。
(3) **对**中文教师**而言**，这本教材非常实用，特别受欢迎。
(4) 职业发展**对**公司的员工**而言**至关重要。

• 为（wèi）(3、4)　to; for

a. 介词，引进动作的受益者和有关的事物，相当于"给""替"。

This is a preposition that introduces the beneficiary of an action. It is similar to "给" or "替".

(1) 当地的21名医生不顾禁令，**为**感染麻疹的孕妇做了堕胎手术，结果遭到逮捕。
(2) 蒂勒当年67岁，他不仅坚持做堕胎手术，还**为**怀孕20周以上的孕妇做晚期堕胎手术，是美国少数几个坚持做晚期堕胎手术的医生之一。

(3) 老师**为**同学们准备了丰盛的午餐。

(4) 他愿意**为**朋友做任何事。

b. 表示目的、原因。可加"了"或"着"。(for the sake of; in order to) This is used to express the objective and purpose of, or to define the cause of, the following clause. "为" is often followed by "了" or "着".

(1) 如果剥夺胎儿的生存权利是不道德的，那么我们应不应该**为了**坚守这种道德意识，而将明明有问题的胎儿也生下来？

(2) **为了**培养下一代，我愿意终身从事教育事业。

(3) 张老师**为**尽快提高我们的中文水平想了很多办法。

(4) 你们不要总是**为**着这么点儿小事吵架。

副课文 Supplementary Text

女青年意外怀孕引起社会关注

近年来，青少年的性和意外怀孕的问题已经引起广泛关注。有调查显示，22%的未婚青年曾发生性行为，其中两成以上的女孩经历了意外怀孕，近九成的意外妊娠最终以人工流产结束，其中20%经历多次流产。

联合国人口基金驻华代表何安瑞说，随着社会价值观的变化，中国青少年不安全性行为、意外怀孕、艾滋病等性传播疾病的风险因素也在增加。联合国人口基金支持中国进行了一项调查。调查的15–24岁的未婚青年男女中，大多数青年人对婚前性行为都持开放的态度，但是其中只有5%非常了解生殖健康问题，15%了解如何避免艾滋病感染。这个调查还显示100个未婚女性中有 4 个会意外怀孕。

在全球范围内，青少年意外怀孕已经成为一个不容忽视的问题。有统计显示，15-19 岁的女孩中，有 1600 万人会生下孩子，怀孕生子造成的并发症是这个年龄的女孩死亡和患病的最主要原因，这一问题在发展中国家尤为严重。而贫困、暴力、童婚、逼婚等因素都是少女怀孕的主要原因；同时，缺乏必要的性知识、人口流动性增加、男女不平等也是造成这种情况的重要因素。

北京东四妇产医院的崔颖大夫告诉记者，她们接诊的流产手术者最小的还不到 17 岁。医生劝告，女孩子们千万别把堕胎当儿戏，否则将会付出沉重的代价：大出血、妇科炎症、终身不孕，甚至死亡。流产除了对身体的伤害之外，对心理的伤害也不可忽视。一位专业人士从医学角度分析，在青春期的青少年性意识开始萌动，期望与异性交往，这是很正常的，但是性教育、性知识的滞后，可能使他们在认识和观念上踏入性的误区，出现各种各样生理、心理上的问题，而这些问题也许会影响人的下半生。

进行必要的性健康教育，让女孩子们懂得如何保护自己是改变这种现象的有效方法。而在中国，性教育缺失的问题仍没有得到解决：青春期性教育至今未被列入课程大纲，学校的教师和家长对性教育讳莫如深，遮遮掩掩，导致青少年对性知识的了解主要来源于网络。

讨论题 Discussion

根据课文内容回答下列问题
(Please answer the following questions based on the text)：

1. 中国年轻人对待"性"的态度与以前有什么不同？这同时造成了哪些问题？
2. 青少年怀孕对女性的身心健康有什么危害？

3. 应该怎么做才能解决青少年怀孕的问题？你有什么好的办法帮助怀孕的青少年？
4. 中国在性教育方面有哪些问题？在你的国家性教育的状况如何？
5. 在你看来，在青春期性意识萌动时，家庭、学校、社会哪方面对一个人的影响是最大，最关键的？如果一个青少年在这方面犯了错，家庭和学校应该如何做？

生词 New Words

1	性行为	性行為	xìngxíngwéi	n.	sexual behavior
2	女孩		nǚhái	n.	girl
3	妊娠		rènshēn	n.	pregnancy, maternity
4	流产	流產	liúchǎn	n./v.	abortion, miscarriage; to abort, to miscarry
5	风险	風險	fēngxiǎn	n.	risk, danger, hazard
6	生殖		shēngzhí	n.	reproduction, procreation
7	不容		bùróng	v.	not tolerate, not allow, not brook
8	忽视	忽視	hūshì	v.	to ignore, to neglect, to overlook
9	患		huàn	v./b.f.	to contract (an illness), to suffer from
10	发展中国家	發展中國家	fāzhǎnzhōng guójiā	n.p.	developing country
11	尤为	尤為	yóuwéi	adv.	especially
12	贫困	貧困	pínkùn	adj.	poor, impoverished
13	童		tóng	b.f./n.	child, under-age servant

第6课
道德还是自由：美国堕胎合法化之争

	简体	繁體	Pinyin		English
14	流动	流動	liúdòng	v./attr.	(of liquid or gas) to flow, to go from place to place; mobile
15	接诊	接診	jiēzhěn	v.	to see and treat patients
16	劝告	勸告	quàngào	v.	to advise, to urge, to recommend
17	儿戏	兒戲	érxì	n.	trifling matter; child's play
18	沉重		chénzhòng	adj.	heavy, serious, critical
19	代价	代價	dàijià	n.	price, cost, expense
20	大出血		dàchūxiě	n.	hematorrhea, heavy bleeding
21	妇科	婦科	fùkē	n.	gynecology
22	炎症		yánzhèng	n.	inflammation, infection
23	伤害	傷害	shānghài	v./n.	to harm, to hurt; injury
24	分析		fēnxī	v./n.	to analyze; analysis
25	萌动	萌動	méngdòng	v.	to germinate, to sprout
26	异性	異性	yìxìng	n.	heterosexual, opposite sex
27	交往		jiāowǎng	v.	to contact, to date, to be in contact with
28	正常		zhèngcháng	adj.	normal
29	性教育		xìngjiàoyù	n.	sex education
30	滞后	滯後	zhìhòu	v.	to lag behind, to delay; hysteresis
31	踏入		tàrù	v(c)	to step into, to enter
32	误区	誤區	wùqū	n.	pitfall, trap, misunderstanding
33	生理		shēnglǐ	n.	physiology, physical
34	缺失		quēshī	n.	lack of, deficiency, deletion, missing
35	青春期		qīngchūnqī	n.	adolescence, puberty
36	大纲	大綱	dàgāng	n.	outline, summary, syllabus

| 37 | 讳莫如深 | 諱莫如深 | huìmòrúshēn | f.e. | to carefully conceal, to avoid mentioning (scandal), to closely guard a secret |
| 38 | 遮遮掩掩 | | zhēzhē-yǎnyǎn | f.e. | to try, to cover up |

专有名词 Proper nouns

1	联合国	聯合國	Liánhéguó	the United Nations (U.N.)
2	何安瑞		Hé Ānruì	Arie Hoekman
3	北京东四妇产医院	北京東四婦產醫院	Běijīng Dōngsì Fùchǎn Yīyuàn	Beijing Dongsi Obstetrical and Gynecological Hospital
4	崔颖	崔穎	Cuī Yǐng	*a person's name*

美国金牌主播因"说谎门"而"下课"[①]

自编自导　　　　新华社发　朱慧卿　作

主课文 Main Text

  2015年2月美国全国广播公司(NBC)的知名主播布莱恩·威廉姆斯被无薪停职六个月,暂时离开主播岗位,成为近来震动美国新闻界的重磅炸弹。威廉姆斯被停职是因为他夸大了自己在伊拉克战争中的采访经历,做了虚假报道。

  2003年伊拉克战争期间,威廉姆斯曾亲往前线做现场报道。他回到美国后,在多个媒体场合说,自己采访时乘坐的直升机遭到了火箭弹的攻击,这

[①] 下课: The original meaning of this expression is "class is over" or "dismiss class". Now it is often used when a person is dismissed or fired from a job or position as a result of unprofessional behavior.

九死一生的战地经历平添了威廉姆斯头顶的光环。此后，他还在晚间节目中回顾了自己的这段光辉经历。但这一次他的谎言被戳穿了。当年的亲历者、飞机工程师雷诺称，威廉姆斯根本没有在他们的飞机上，他们迫降一小时后才看到威廉姆斯赶过来。其他老兵也证实了事情的真相。

威廉姆斯随后在新闻节目中道歉。他说这是出于记忆误差："我在回顾12年前发生的事件时犯了一个错误。"但是这一道歉显然没有平息外界的批评声音。事件发生后人们不仅对威廉姆斯有关伊拉克的报道产生怀疑，而且披露出他2005年报道卡特里娜飓风灾难的时候也可能夸大了事实。据报道，威廉姆斯当时在新奥尔良报道的时候说他从饭店看到尸体漂过，但是当地民众质疑说，他的饭店所在的地区并没有被水淹。

该事件不仅使威廉姆斯的可信度受到了质疑，也使人们对NBC新闻频道的操守和审查提出了批评。美国收视率最高的三大电视新闻节目是NBC、ABC和CBS，而威廉姆斯主持的晚间新闻节目长期以来收视率最高，吸引了近一千万美国观众。据CNN报道，他的丑闻曝光后，NBC晚间新闻收视人数流失了七十万。NBC首席执行官斯蒂芬·伯克就此事发表声明称："布莱恩的行为破坏了数百万美国人给予NBC新闻频道的信任……他的行为不可原谅，停职是一个严厉且恰当的处罚。"威廉姆斯在写给NBC的一封信中说："在我的职业生涯中，我一直追踪报道新闻，然而我现在痛苦地意识到，由于我自己的行为，我本人成为了新闻焦点。"

这个事件引起了美国各大媒体对新闻界的职业道德和诚信的热烈讨论。有人认为这是记者们惯用的伎俩，就是通过谎言推动一个话题。有人指责NBC新闻部门失职，因为这个故事足够好，所以没人愿意去核实它是否真实；即使造假，名主播受罚的可能性很小。还有人认为电视台乐于新闻造"神"：知名主播出现在战场、总统身边，或是灾难现场，其曝光率高过好莱坞名人。

一个值得探讨的问题是，事业上如此辉煌的著名记者为什么要说如此低级的谎话？一般认为，威廉姆斯的事业如日中天，完全不需要对真相进行涂脂抹粉增加自己的光彩。这一"说谎门"事件带来的最重要启示是，身居高位的人即使有了至高无上的地位和荣誉，仍然可能通过造假提高自己的声誉，以便让人更加仰慕、崇拜他。

这次事件表明，市场经济下即使是商业媒体也必须以真相和诚信为根本。另外，社交媒体在这次事件中的作用值得关注。今天的社交媒体给观众提供了监督身居高位者的机会。过去，威廉姆斯不止一次在公开场合讲述同样的故事，都被忽略了。这次，当年的一名直升机机组人员在脸书上指出他的错误后，在极短时间内引起公众讨论和媒体关注，揭示出真相。最后，这一事件还说明，舆论监督对任何人都不能例外，尤其是拥有巨大话语权的显赫人士。

讨论题 Discussion

根据课文内容回答下列问题

(Please answer the following questions based on the text)

1. 美国全国广播公司的知名主播布莱恩·威廉姆斯做了什么样的虚假报道？
2. 在威廉姆斯关于卡特里娜飓风灾难的报道中又有什么不真实的地方？
3. 威廉姆斯的"说谎门"对美国全国广播公司造成了什么危害？
4. 文章中分析威廉姆斯说谎的原因是什么？你同意吗？
5. 威廉姆斯的说谎事件说明了什么问题？在你看来，新闻职业最重要的职业操守是什么？为什么？

生词 New Words

1	金牌		jīnpái	n.	gold medal
2	主播		zhǔbō	n.	anchor (TV)
3	说谎	說謊	shuō huǎng	v.o.	to tell a lie, to lie
4	薪		xīn	b.f.	salary, wages
5	停职	停職	tíng zhí	v.o.	to suspend sb. from his duties
6	震动	震動	zhèndòng	v.	to shake, to shock, to vibrate
7	界		jiè	b.f.	boundary, border, circles, world
8	磅		bàng	n./m(n)	pound
9	炸弹	炸彈	zhàdàn	n.	bomb, bombshell
10	夸大	誇大	kuādà	v.	to exaggerate, to overstate, to magnify
11	虚假	虛假	xūjiǎ	adj.	false, sham, deceitful
12	亲	親	qīn	b.f.	in person, personally
13	前线	前線	qiánxiàn	n.	front, frontline, battlefront
14	乘坐		chéngzuò	v.	to ride (in a vehicle), to embark
15	直升机	直昇機	zhíshēngjī	n.	helicopter, copter
16	火箭弹	火箭彈	huǒjiàndàn	n.	rocket, missile
17	九死一生		jiǔsǐ-yīshēng	f.e.	a hairbreadth escape; barely escape
18	战地	戰地	zhàndì	n.	battle field
19	平添		píngtiān	v.	to add sth. unexpectedly
20	头顶	頭頂	tóudǐng	n.	the top of the head
21	光环	光環	guānghuán	n.	aura, glory, ring of light
22	晚间	晚間	wǎnjiān	n.	evening, night

Lesson 7

美国金牌主播因"说谎门"而"下课"

23	回顾	回顧	huígù	v.	to review, to retrospect, to look back
24	谎言	謊言	huǎngyán	n.	lie, falsehood
25	戳穿		chuōchuān	v.	to pierce through, to expose, to reveal
26	历	歷	lì	b.f.	to go through, to undergo, to experience
27	迫降		pòjiàng	v.	to have a forced landing, to have an emergency landing
28	老兵		lǎobīng	n.	veterans, veteran soldiers
29	真相		zhēnxiàng	n.	facts, truth
30	随后	隨後	suíhòu	adv.	soon afterward, subsequently, then
31	误差	誤差	wùchā	n.	error
32	平息		píngxī	v.	to quiet down, to subside, to suppress
33	外界		wàijiè	n.	outside, the outside world, external
34	披露		pīlù	v.	to reveal, to disclose, to publish, to announce
35	飓风	颶風	jùfēng	n.	hurricane
36	尸体	屍體	shītǐ	n.	dead body, corpse, remains
37	漂		piāo	v.	to drift, to float about
38	淹		yān	v./b.f.	to flood, to submerge, to inundate
39	可信		kěxìn	adj.	credible, believable, trustworthy
40	操守		cāoshǒu	n.	work ethic, personal integrity
41	晚间新闻	晚間新聞	wǎnjiān xīnwén	n.p.	evening news
42	流失		liúshī	v.	to run off, to be washed away, to flow away
43	给予	給予	jǐyǔ	v.	to give, to render, to offer
44	信任		xìnrèn	v.	to trust, to have confidence in, to believe in
45	追踪	追蹤	zhuīzōng	v.	to follow the trail of, to track, to trace
46	本人		běnrén	pron.	oneself, I (me, myself); in person

47	诚信	誠信	chéngxìn	n.	sincerity and honesty
48	惯	慣	guàn	v.	to be used to, to be accustomed to
49	伎俩	伎倆	jìliǎng	n.	trick, maneuver, illicit means
50	指责	指責	zhǐzé	v.	to blame, to accuse, to find fault with
51	失职	失職	shī zhí	v.o.	to neglect one's duty, dereliction of duty
52	核实	核實	héshí	v.	to verify, to check
53	造假		zào jiǎ	v.o.	to fake, to make fake products
54	受罚	受罰	shòu fá	v.o.	to be punished, to receive punishment
55	乐于	樂於	lèyú	v.	to be happy to, to take delight in
56	战场	戰場	zhànchǎng	n.	battlefield, battlefront
57	名人		míngrén	n.	celebrity, famous person
58	辉煌	輝煌	huīhuáng	adj.	brilliant, splendid, glorious
59	低级	低級	dījí	adj.	low level, elementary, vulgar
60	谎话	謊話	huǎnghuà	n.	lie, falsehood
61	如日中天		rúrì-zhōngtiān	f.e.	at the apex of one's power or career
62	涂脂抹粉	塗脂抹粉	túzhī-mǒfěn	f.e.	to apply facial makeup, to prettify
63	光彩		guāngcǎi	n.	luster, splendor, glory
64	居		jū	v./b.f.	to reside, to be (in a certain position), to occupy (a place)
65	高位		gāowèi	n.	high position or post
66	至高无上	至高無上	zhìgāo-wúshàng	f.e.	supreme, sovereign
67	荣誉	榮譽	róngyù	n.	honor, glory, credit
68	声誉	聲譽	shēngyù	n.	reputation, fame, prestige
69	以便		yǐbiàn	conj.	so that, in order to, so as to

Lesson 7

第7课
美国金牌主播因"说谎门"而"下课"

70	仰慕		yǎngmù	v./n.	to admire, to look up to; adoration
71	不止		bùzhǐ	v.	to be more than, to exceed, not limited to
72	机组	機組	jīzǔ	n.	flight crew, aircrew
73	揭示		jiēshì	v.	to reveal, to bring to light
74	话语	話語	huàyǔ	n.	speech, utterance
75	显赫	顯赫	xiǎnhè	adj.	illustrious, celebrated, eminent

专有名词 Proper nouns

1	全国广播公司	全國廣播公司	Quánguó Guǎngbō Gōngsī	National Broadcasting Company (NBC)
2	布莱恩·威廉姆斯	布萊恩·威廉姆斯	Bùlái'ēn Wēiliánmǔsī	Brian Williams
3	伊拉克		Yīlākè	Iraq
4	雷诺	雷諾	Léinuò	Reynolds
5	卡特里娜		Kǎtèlǐnà	Katrina
6	新奥尔良	新奧爾良	Xīn'ào'ěrliáng	New Orleans
7	斯蒂芬·伯克		Sīdìfēn Bókè	Stephen Burks

词语注释 Vocabulary and Grammar explanations

语素 (morphemes)

—薪：薪水；工资。(salary; wages; pay)

> 例 无薪 停薪 半薪 全薪 年薪 工薪 月薪 评薪

107

-界：职业、工作或性别等相同的一些社会成员的总体。(circles; fields; world)

> 例 新闻界　体育界　文艺界　教育界　电影界　文学界　外交界
> 工业界

-弹：内装爆炸物，具有破坏和杀伤能力的东西。(bullet; bomb; missile)

> 例 火箭弹　导弹　炸弹　原子弹　核弹　手榴弹　子弹　飞弹　炮弹
> 枪弹　流弹　信号弹

-机：机器；飞机。(machine; engine; airplane)

> 例 直升机　饮水机　碎冰机　割草机　战斗机　洗衣机　烘干机
> 电视机　运输机　客机

亲-：亲自。(in person; personally)

> 例 亲历　亲笔　亲传　亲临　亲口　亲身　亲生　亲手　亲眼　亲知
> 亲自

失-：1. 没有达到目的。(to lose; to miss)

> 例 失职　失策　失察　失利　失望　失意

2. 改变常态。(to deviate from the normal)

> 例 失声　失色　失态　失神　失密

受-：接受；遭受；忍受。(to receive; to accept; to suffer from; to endure)

> 例 受罚　受潮　受害　受贿　受审　受阻　受训　受洗　受聘　受奖
> 受骗　受气　受伤　受用　受制

108

-门：丑闻；事件。(-gate)

 说谎门 水门 电邮门 拉链门 捐款门 艳照门 伊朗门 棱镜门

● 四字格和成语 (four-character expressions and idioms)

● **九死一生**

指死的可能性远大于活的可能性，但终于脱险。形容经历很大危险而幸存。

This literally means that there is a ninety percent chance of dying and a ten percent chance of surviving, so a very slim chance of escape; it indicates that a person escapes or survives from an extremely dangerous situation.

 (1) 他回到美国后，在多个媒体场合说，自己采访时乘坐的直升机遭到了火箭弹的攻击，这**九死一生**的战地经历平添了威廉姆斯头顶的光环。
(2) 他为了救朋友，冒着**九死一生**的危险，一个人去和绑匪谈判。
(3) 同船伙伴都葬身大海，只有他一个人**九死一生**，回到家乡。
(4) 很多人为了国家，**九死一生**，人民永远不会忘记他们。

● **如日中天**

意思是好像太阳正处于天空正当中，比喻事物正发展到十分兴盛的阶段。

This literally means that sun is in the middle of the sky at high noon, it is used as a metaphor to indicate "someone is at the peak of his /her power or career" or "something is at the peak period of thriving and flourishing."

 (1) 一般认为，威廉姆斯的事业**如日中天**，完全不需要对真相进行涂脂抹粉增加自己的光彩。

(2) 他在电影界这几年如日中天，红得发紫。

(3) 现在互联网业如日中天，硅谷每天创造64个百万富翁，其中许多是年轻人，多半又都是男性。

(4) 可以说有了这些忠实的歌迷的支持，他的事业才更加如日中天。

- **涂脂抹粉**

涂胭脂，抹香粉；原指妇女打扮，修饰容貌，现在多比喻对丑恶事物进行掩饰美化。

This literally means "to apply rouge and face powder"; originally it referred to the act of women applying their make-up, but now it is mostly used as a metaphor for prettifying ugly or bad things or scandals.

(1) 一般认为，威廉姆斯的事业如日中天，完全不需要对真相进行涂脂抹粉增加自己的光彩。

(2) 美丽的女人用不着涂脂抹粉，特别是在学校读书的女孩子。

(3) 豪华车里坐着一些衣着鲜艳、涂脂抹粉的女人。

(4) 侵略者竭力为自己的侵略行径涂脂抹粉，妄图逃脱世界舆论的谴责。

- **至高无上**

至高：最高。高到顶点，再也没有更高的了。

"至高" means "the highest". The whole idiom means "the highest point and nothing is taller than it".

(1) 这一"说谎门"事件带来的最重要启示是，身居高位的人即使有了至高无上的地位和荣誉，仍然可能通过造假提高自己的声誉，以便让人更加仰慕、崇拜他。

(2) 希腊人在数学史上有至高无上的地位。

(3) 虽然有**至高无上**的权力，但是他也对此事无可奈何。
(4) 这些东西对于你**至高无上**，对于别人可能一钱不值。

● 虚词及句型 (function words and sentence patterns)

如此　so, such; in this way, like that

副词，意思是"这样"，表示程度深。"如此"后面常带形容词或动词，而且一般是双音节或多音节。如果它后面带的是单音节形容词，那么形容词之前要加"之"字，使之成为双音节。

This is an adverb that means "so, such" and indicates a higher degree or deeper extent. "如此" is often followed by an adjective or verb, which generally is multisyllabic or disyllabic. If the following adjective is monosyllabic, then a "之" must be added to make it disyllabic.

(1) 一个值得探讨的问题是，事业上如此辉煌的著名记者为什么要说**如此**低级的谎话？
(2) 没想到你的内心世界**如此**丰富，以前对你的了解太少了。
(3) 真的非常感谢你们家**如此**热情周到地照顾我们这么长时间。
(4) 中国**如此**之大，人口**如此**之多，做这个国家的领导人太不容易了。

以便　so that; in order to; so as to; for the purpose of

连词，连接两个分句。用在后一个分句的开头，表示使下文所说的目的容易实现。主语相同时，后一分句从不出现主语。

This is a conjunction used to connect two clauses in a complex sentence. It usually occurs at the beginning of the second clause to achieve the goal indicated in that clause. If the subjects of the complex sentence are the same, the subject is omitted in the second clause.

(1) 这一"说谎门"事件带来的最重要启示是，身居高位的人即使有了至高无上的地位和荣誉，仍然可能通过造假提高自己的声誉，**以便**让人更加仰慕、崇拜他。
(2) 请你在黑板上把字写得大一点儿，**以便**后边的同学们看清楚。
(3) 你把地址留给我吧，**以便**以后联系。
(4) 把安全出口的杂物搬走，**以便**日后发生火灾逃生时通行无阻。

- **尤其** especially, particularly

副词，表示更进一步，强调在全体中或者与其他事物比较时，特别突出，有"更加""特别"的意思。用在动词或形容词前，但是如果与"是"组合成"尤其是"，可直接放在名词、代词或分句前。

This is an adverb that indicates something or someone is "a step further"; it emphasizes an outstanding thing or person when compared with other things or persons, meaning "especially" or "particularly". This expression is used before verbs and adjectives; however, if used with "是" as in "尤其是", it can also occur before nouns, pronouns, and clauses.

(1) 最后，这一事件还说明，舆论监督对任何人都不能例外，**尤其**是拥有巨大话语权的显赫人士。
(2) 我最喜欢交朋友了，**尤其**是同龄的朋友。
(3) 今年的天气都很热，**尤其**是今天，气温都达35摄氏度了。
(4) 你们的想法都很好，**尤其**是小明的，很有独创性。
(5) 我很喜欢看书，**尤其**喜欢看历史传记。

副课文 Supplementary Text

三人行，必有一自媒体

读到一本好书，立刻摘出精彩段落，附上感悟，发微信分享到朋友圈；逛街遇到突发事件或趣闻，第一时间掏手机录视频，上传网络，广而告之。互联网时代，随着智能手机的普及以及微博、微信的迅速发展，越来越多的人成为"自媒体人"。人称当今社会是"三人行，必有一自媒体"的年代："人人都是发布者，个个都有麦克风。"

"自媒体"也称"公民媒体"，是指普通市民或机构组织在任何时间、任何地点，以任何方式访问网络，提供并分享他们的真实看法和自身新闻。自媒体包括但不限于个人微博、个人日志、个人主页等，其中最有代表性的平台美国是脸书和推特，中国是Qzone、新浪微博、腾讯微博、人人网、微信公众平台等。当前，以微博为代表的自媒体，已成为网络传播最活跃的主体和新兴舆论场。网络自媒体的数量庞大，其拥有者也大多为"草根"平民，网络的隐匿性给了网民"随心所欲"的空间。

自媒体的传播潜力和效益是惊人的。2015年初，中国著名新闻人柴静的自媒体视频《穹顶之下》以一己之力，掀起了从国家领导人到街头巷尾，乃至整个中国社会对雾霾的关注。该视频总播放量达到了1.17亿，成为2015年传播最广、影响最大的视频。清华大学新闻与传播学院博士生导师沈阳教授介绍了一个惊人的数字：据调查，每个中国人平均每天摸手机150次。这就意味着自媒体有着巨大的传播潜力。而"今日头条"首席执行官张一鸣也表示，在"今日头条"的平台上，由自媒体创作的内容已经占到了一半的比例，他认为这个比例还可能增加。

自媒体作为一种新型媒体已经参与了商业运营、专业培训、学术讨论、科技普及、抢险救灾、维护公共秩序、道德监督和促进社会公益等多种社会活动。山西忻州民警发现一名与父母走失的3岁男童。警方通过自媒体为小孩找父母的信息转发超过6500次，迅速帮孩子找到了家人。安徽老人胡玉娣90岁高龄还得照顾53岁脑瘫的儿子。安庆师范学院新闻专业的学生程江涛在寒假实习时为老人拍摄了一组照片，通过网络发布，同时设立网络公益项目，二十多天时间里收到了5万多条评论，1227名网友为老人捐款50050.69元人民币。

门槛儿低、包容性强、内容丰富，网络的最大好处在于人人平等，人人享有话语权。事件发生后，大家各抒己见，百家争鸣。不过，在为大家提供良好传播平台的同时，"人人自媒体"也带来了不少伤害，发布便利、扩散快等优势也成为一把双刃剑：譬如谣言满天飞，再迅速发酵，公众不明真相先入为主，恶劣影响一旦产生便很难消除等。自媒体的完善有待于政府出台更具有操作性的互联网细则，来保证它更加有序的发展。

讨论题 Discussion

根据课文内容回答下列问题
(Please answer the following questions based on the text)

1. "自媒体人"指的是哪种人？如果你也是，说说你的"自媒体"经历。
2. 美国和中国有代表性的自媒体有哪些？你常用哪些？
3. 为什么人们会越来越多的使用自媒体？
4. 自媒体的影响力怎么样？课文举了哪些例子说明？
5. 总结一下自媒体的正面和负面的影响力。说说你的看法。

生词 New Words

1	段落	duànluò	n.	paragraph
2	附	fù	v.	to add, to attach, to enclose

3	突发	突發	tūfā	v.	to burst out or occur suddenly
4	趣闻	趣聞	qùwén	n.	interesting news, anecdotes
5	第一时间	第一時間	dì yī shíjiān	n.p	at the first moment, immediately
6	广	廣	guǎng	adj.	wide, vast, extensive
7	麦克风	麥克風	màikèfēng	n.	microphone
8	限于	限於	xiànyú	v.	to be confined to, to be limited to
9	日志	日誌	rìzhì	n.	journal, daily record, log
10	主页	主頁	zhǔyè	n.	homepage
11	平台	平臺	píngtái	n.	movable platform; terrace, flat roof
12	庞大	龐大	pángdà	adj.	big, huge, immense, enormous
13	草根		cǎogēn	n.	grass roots
14	潜力	潛力	qiánlì	n.	latent capacity, potential, potentiality
15	效益		xiàoyì	n.	effectiveness, beneficial result, benefit
16	惊人	驚人	jīngrén	adj.	astonishing, amazing, alarming
17	年初		niánchū	n.	beginning of the year
18	穹顶	穹頂	qióngdǐng	n.	dome, vault
19	一己		yìjǐ	n.	self, oneself
20	街头巷尾	街頭巷尾	jiētóu-xiàngwěi	f.e.	street corners and alleys, everywhere
21	雾霾	霧霾	wùmái	n.	fog and haze, smog
22	播放		bōfàng	v.	to broadcast, to transmit, to show
23	博士生		bóshìshēng	n.	doctoral candidate, Ph.d students
24	导师	導師	dǎoshī	n.	tutor, teacher, supervisor, mentor
25	培训	培訓	péixùn	v./n.	to cultivate, to train; training
26	抢险	搶險	qiǎng xiǎn	v.o.	to rush to rescue, to rush to deal with an emergency

27	救灾	救災	jiù zāi	v.o.	to provide disaster relief, to send relief to a disaster area
28	民警		mínjǐng	n.	people's police, policeman
29	走失		zǒushī	v.	to be lost, to be missing
30	警方		jǐngfāng	n.	the police
31	转发	轉發	zhuǎnfā	v.	to repost, to relay, to retransmit
32	家人		jiārén	n.	family members
33	高龄	高齡	gāolíng	n.	advanced age, venerable age
34	脑	腦	nǎo	n./b.f.	brain, head, mind
35	瘫	癱	tān	v.	to be paralyzed
36	实习	實習	shíxí	v.	to practice, to do fieldwork
37	拍摄	拍攝	pāishè	v.	to shoot (a photograph, movie, etc.)
38	设立	設立	shèlì	v.	to establish, to set up, to found
39	捐款		juān kuǎn	v.o.	to donate money, to contribute funds
40	门槛儿	門檻兒	ménkǎnr	n.	threshold
41	享有		xiǎngyǒu	v.	to enjoy (rights, privileges, etc.)
42	各抒己见	各抒己見	gè shū jǐ jiàn	f.e.	each expresses his own views
43	百家争鸣	百家爭鳴	bǎi jiā zhēng míng	f.e.	contention of a hundred schools of thought, to let a hundred schools of thought contend
44	便利		biànlì	adj./v.	convenient, easy; to facilitate
45	刃		rèn	b.f./v.	blade; to kill with a sword or knife
46	剑	劍	jiàn	n.	sword
47	譬如		pìrú	v.	for example, for instance, such as
48	谣言	謠言	yáoyán	n.	rumor, canard
49	发酵	發酵	fājiào	v.	to ferment

50	不明		bùmíng	v./ adj.	to fail to understand, not clear, unknown
51	先入为主	先入為主	xiān rù wéi zhǔ	f.e.	be prejudiced by first impressions; first impressions are firmly entrenched
52	一旦		yídàn	conj.	in case (something happens), once
53	细则	細則	xìzé	n.	detailed rules and regulations
54	有序		yǒuxù	v.	to be in order

专有名词 Proper nouns

1	推特		Tuītè	Twitter
2	新浪		Xīnlàng	Sina, *a Chinese website*
3	腾讯	騰訊	Téngxùn	Tencent, *a Chinese company*
4	人人网	人人網	Rénrén Wǎng	RENN, *Chinese Facebook*
5	微信		Wēixìn	WeChat
6	柴静	柴靜	Chái Jìng	*a person's name*
7	沈阳	瀋陽	Shěn Yáng	*a person's name*
8	今日头条	今日頭條	Jīnrì Tóutiáo	Today's Headline News
9	张一鸣	張一鳴	Zhāng Yīmíng	*a person's name*
10	忻州		Xīnzhōu	Xinzhou City in Shanxi Province
11	安徽		Ānhuī	Anhui (province)
12	胡玉娣		Hú Yùdì	*a person's name*
13	安庆师范学院	安慶師範學院	Ānqìng Shīfàn Xuéyuàn	Anqing Teachers College
14	程江涛	程江濤	Chéng Jiāngtāo	*a person's name*

第8课 外媒热议：中国开放"二胎"政策

落地　　　　　　　　新华社发　徐骏　作

主课文 Main Text

2013年11月15日，中国政府决定实施"单独二胎"的政策，即：一方是独生子女的夫妇可生育两个孩子。2015年底，经过调研和论证，中国政府再次调整生育政策，决定全面放开"二胎"，结束了实施了三十六年的独生子女政策。过去三十多年，外媒对中国的计生政策褒贬不一，但得出的结论大同小异——独生子女政策已重塑中国社会。当然，人们也常把中国与"老龄化社会"的日本相提并论。"二胎"政策的出台引起了外媒热议。

《华尔街日报》网络头条文章说，计划生育政策自从1980年开始实施以来一直受到官方的称赞，说该政策遏制了人口大规模增长。但经济学家们说，这样的政策可能损害中国的竞争优势，减少未来的劳动者数量，并给中国的社会福利体系带来更大的压力。中国改变生育政策，可能是一个明智的理念：这对中国保持经济增长和政权稳定不可缺少。有美国媒体猜测说，开放二胎会稳定中国房价市场，避免房价下降；美国农场主的粮食出口也会增加，因为中国未来会进口更多粮食。

一直关注中国计划生育政策的英国人口老龄化学会学者皮尔·波特认为，近四十年的计划生育政策可以说是中国人口战略史上的成功一步，它通过降低生育率保障了国民的基本生活，也让中国女性有了更多参与社会活动的时间。但是这个政策如果一成不变，其负面效应会很明显。一旦中国进入老龄化发展阶段，就会在国际上越来越缺少竞争力。他举例说，北京、上海等城市数以千万计的老龄群体越来越依赖国家的养老金生活，这让政府的公共项目开支不得不进一步缩减，让社会公共福利质量出现下降，同时会导致城乡人口发展不均衡的现象加重。

路透社评论说，开放二胎，从长期来看，将解决生育率低的问题；从短期来看，婴儿潮的到来将拉动相关食品、玩具、母婴医疗、儿童服饰、家用汽车、教育培训等行业的发展。

新加坡《联合早报》说：两个孩子的好处显而易见，只生一个孩子，不只是父母心疼子女太孤单，一些独生子女的性格特征也令人担忧。1979年后出生的独生子女"互信程度较低、倾向于规避风险、情绪上更为悲观"。空巢老人缺少精神关爱，也是"一胎"政策所造成的问题。家庭养老一向是中国人传统的养老模式，随着父辈们逐渐迈入老年，中国第一代独生子女已然在面临赡养老人的压力。

不过，政策是放开了，是否要享受这一权利，相当一部分家庭也许还要再斟酌一番。随着人们的价值取向发生转变，中国民众生二胎的积极性已大不如前，而且添丁不仅仅是"添双筷子"，城镇居民的生活成本水涨船高，二胎显然不是人人都能"消费"得起。

据香港《南华早报》2013年11月23日报道：上海父母对开放二胎反

应冷淡。新浪网对 1200 位上海居民实施的调查发现，70% 的接受调查者不想要二胎。其中，24% 的人明确表示只要一个孩子，46% 的人表示"可能"会只要一个孩子。抚养孩子的成本似乎是让人们犹豫的主要原因。养育一个孩子的负担已经够重了，抚养两个孩子超过了多数家庭的经济能力。据粗略估算，在上海将一个孩子从出生供到大学毕业至少需要100万元人民币。一些头胎为儿子的年轻夫妇更担心二胎还是男孩。上海人认为，养活男孩的成本远远高于养活女孩，因为等男孩长大结婚时，得承担为他们买房的负担。

《纽约时报》说，2013 年底实施"单独二胎"以来，截止到 2015 年 5 月，中国全国共有约 145 万对夫妻申请生育二胎，只占所有符合"单独二胎"夫妻数目的 12% 左右，这让人口学家和政策制定者颇为失望。如今，中国实施全面二胎政策，显然是希望婴儿潮会为国家提供更多的劳动力，同时鼓励人们更多地消费。

讨论题 Discussion

根据课文内容回答下列问题

(Please answer the following questions based on the text):

1. 什么是中国的"二胎"政策？这一政策与以前的计划生育政策有什么不同？
2. 中国实施计划生育政策的好处和坏处是什么？中国为什么要全面开放"二胎"？
3. 计划生育政策对独生子女的成长和他们的家庭有什么影响？
4. 据这篇文章说，为什么很多中国家庭不想生第二胎？
5. 你对中国的计划生育政策及开放"二胎"有什么看法？

Lesson 8

第 8 课
外媒热议：中国开放"二胎"政策

生词 New Words

1	单独	單獨	dāndú	adv./attr	alone, solely, by oneself; here it is an abbreviation, meaning "one side of the married couple is a single child".
2	胎		tāi	n./m(n)	fetus, embryo, baby
3	调整	調整	tiáozhěng	v.	to adjust, to tinker up
4	计生	計生	jìshēng	abbr.	family planning (about having children)
5	褒贬	褒貶	bāobiǎn	v.	to appraise, to judge
6	得出		déchū	v(c)	to reach (a conclusion), to obtain (a result)
7	大同小异	大同小異	dàtóngxiǎoyì	f.e.	much the same with only minor differences
8	塑		sù	v.	to model, to mould
9	老龄	老齡	lǎolíng	n.	aging, elderly people, old age
10	相提并论	相提並論	xiāngtí-bìnglùn	f.e.	to mention in the same breath, to place on a par
11	经济学	經濟學	jīngjìxué	n.	economics
12	明智		míngzhì	adj.	sagacious, wise, sensible
13	政权	政權	zhèngquán	n.	political power, state power, regime
14	不可		bùkě	aux.	should not, must not
15	猜测	猜測	cāicè	v.	to guess, to conjecture, to surmise
16	农场	農場	nóngchǎng	n.	farm, ranch, homestead
17	战略	戰略	zhànlüè	n.	strategy, tactic
18	一成不变	一成不變	yìchéngbúbiàn	f.e.	nothing ever changes
19	竞争力	競爭力	jìngzhēnglì	n.	competitive power or strength
20	举例	舉例	jǔ lì	v.o.	to give an example, to sample

21	计	計	jì	v.	to calculate, to count
22	养老金	養老金	yǎnglǎojīn	n.	pension
23	开支	開支	kāizhī	v./n.	to spend, to expend; expenses, expenditure
24	城乡	城鄉	chéngxiāng	n.	city and countryside, urban and rural
25	均衡		jūnhéng	adj.	balanced, even
26	加重		jiāzhòng	v.	to make or become heavier
27	婴儿	嬰兒	yīng'ér	n.	baby, infant
28	食品		shípǐn	n.	food, foodstuff
29	玩具		wánjù	n.	toy, plaything
30	儿童	兒童	értóng	n.	children
31	培训	培訓	péixùn	v.	to train
32	显而易见	顯而易見	xiǎn'éryìjiàn	f.e.	obviously, evidently, clearly
33	心疼		xīnténg	v.	to love dearly, to make one's heart ache, to feel sorry
34	孤单	孤單	gūdān	adj.	lonely, friendless, alone
35	特征	特徵	tèzhēng	n.	characteristic, feature, property
36	互		hù	adv.	mutually; mutual, each other
37	规避	規避	guībì	v.	to evade, to dodge, to elude
38	悲观	悲觀	bēiguān	adj.	pessimistic
39	巢		cháo	n.	nest of a bird, nest, beehive
40	关爱	關愛	guān'ài	v.	to express solicitude for the wellbeing of, to concern and love
41	养老	養老	yǎng lǎo	v.o.	to provide for the aged, to live out one's life in retirement
42	父辈	父輩	fùbèi	n.	elder generation

Lesson 8

外媒热议：中国开放"二胎"政策

43	老年		lǎonián	n.	old age, elderly, aging
44	已然		yǐrán	adv./v.	already; to be already so
45	赡养	贍養	shànyǎng	v.	to support, to provide for
46	斟酌		zhēnzhuó	v.	to consider, to deliberate
47	取向		qǔxiàng	n.	orientation
48	添丁		tiān dīng	v.o.	to have a baby born into the family
49	不仅仅	不僅僅	bùjǐnjǐn	conj.	not only
50	居民		jūmín	n.	resident, inhabitant
51	水涨船高	水漲船高	shuǐzhǎng chuángāo	f.e.	particulars improve as general situation does; all ships rise with the tide
52	冷淡		lěngdàn	adj.	cold, indifferent
53	犹豫	猶豫	yóuyù	adj.	hesitate, be irresolute, wavering
54	粗略		cūlüè	adv.	roughly, approximately
55	估算		gūsuàn	v.	to rough estimate, to reckon
56	远远	遠遠	yuǎnyuǎn	r.f.	far away, distant
57	截止		jiézhǐ	v(c)	to end, to close
58	约	約	yuē	adv.	about, approximately
59	符合		fúhé	v.	to accord with, to tally with
60	夫妻		fūqī	n.	husband and wife, spouse
61	数目	數目	shùmù	n.	number, amount
62	人口		rénkǒu	n.	population
63	制定	製定	zhìdìng	v.	to formulate, to lay down, to draw up
64	失望		shīwàng	adj.	disappointed

| 65 | 消费 | 消費 | xiāofèi | v. | to consume, to spend |

专有名词 Proper nouns

1	皮尔·波特	皮爾·波特	Pí'ěr Bōtè	Bill Porter
2	联合早报	聯合早報	Liánhé Zǎobào	*Lianhe Zaobao* (a Singapore newspaper)
3	路透社		Lùtòushè	Reuters News Agency
4	南华早报	南華早報	Nánhuá Zǎobào	*South China Morning Post*

词语注释 Vocabulary and Grammar explanations

语素 (morphemes)

-研/研-：深入地探求。(to research; to study; to investigate)

> 例 调研　科研　钻研　研究　研讨　研发　研习

-媒/媒-：使双方发生关系的人或事物。(intermediary; to mediate between people and things)

> 例 外媒　官媒　传媒　自媒　媒体　媒介　媒婆　媒人　做媒　保媒

-价/价-：商品所值的钱数。(price of merchandise)

> 例 房价　物价　市价　车价　减价　加价　提价　价格　价位　价目

-减/减-：1. 由原有数量中去掉一部分。(to subtract from the original amount)

> 例 缩减　精减　削减　裁减

124

2. 降低程度，衰退。(to diminish; to reduce; to subside)

例 减少　减低　减弱　减除　减去　减掉

-养/养-：1. 供给生活品。(to raise; to provide for)

例 赡养　抚养　养家　养活

2. 滋补，保护，使看起来舒服。(to nurture; to protect; to make more pleasing to the eye)

例 养颜　养眼　保养　营养　休养

3. 教育。(to educate)

例 培养　教养

● 四字格和成语 (four-character expressions and idioms)

● ~~不一

不一致的意思。常见的形式是：对立的形容词/名词＋"不一"。(This means "not consistent" or "not the same"; the often used form is: contrastive adjectives or nouns＋"不一".)

例 褒贬不一　毁誉不一　看法不一　意见不一　做法不一

例 (1) 外媒对中国的计生政策褒贬不一。
(2) 专家们对这本书毁誉不一。

(3) 观众对《私人定制》这个电影褒贬不一。
(4) 美国民众对奥巴马总统毁誉不一。

- **大同小异**

异：差异。大体相同，略有差异。("异" means different or difference. This expression means "largely identical but with minor differences".)

(1) 外媒对中国的计生政策褒贬不一，但得出的结论大同小异。
(2) 我们的看法大同小异，基本上是一致的。
(3) 欧盟跟美国在很多国际争端上的态度和做法大同小异。
(4) 这两本教材大同小异，没有太大的区别。

- **相提并论**

相提：相对照；并：齐。把不同的人或不同的事放在一起谈论或看待。("相提" means "to compare or mention two things"; "并" means "together". This expression means "to be mentioned in the same breath".)

(1) 人们也常把中国与"老龄化社会"的日本相提并论。
(2) 这是两个完全不同的概念，不能相提并论。
(3) 人们常把中国现在的考试升学制度跟古代的科举考试相提并论。
(4) 小李比小王差远了，怎么可以相提并论？

- **一成不变**

成：制定，形成。一经形成，不再改变。("成" means "to establish; to take shape". This expression means that once a job is done, or a system is established, things will remain the same, and nothing will have been altered or changed.)

(1) 这个政策如果一成不变，其负面效应会很明显。
(2) 自然界和人类社会都在不断地变化，没有什么是一成不变的。
(3) 你这种认为事物一成不变的看法是错误的。
(4) 人不是一成不变的。在我们的耐心帮助下，他一定会改变的！

- 显而易见

形容事情或道理很明显，极容易看清楚。(obvious, evident)

 (1) 生两个孩子的好处显而易见。
(2) 小李换了一个离小王近点儿的工作。他这样做的目的显而易见，就是想跟小王见面更容易一些。
(3) 环境污染给我们带来的问题显而易见，不需要我在这儿列举了。
(4) 北京的交通存在着很多问题，这是显而易见，人人皆知的。

- 水涨船高

水位升高，船身也随之浮起。比喻事物随着它所凭借的基础的提高而增长提高。("When the river rises, the boat floats high"; this expression is usually used as a metaphor for things becoming elevated or improved because of the foundation they are based on.)

 (1) 城镇居民的生活成本水涨船高，二胎显然不是人人都能"消费"得起。
(2) 家长都想给孩子选个好学校，认为水涨船高，好的学习环境可以把孩子带动起来。
(3) 这几年很多外地人都在北京买房子，水涨船高，就把北京的房价炒起来了。
(4) 人人都想上有名的大学，结果是水涨船高，把这些大学的学费哄抬起来了。

虚词及句型 (function words and sentence patterns)

- **一直** continuously; always; all along; all the way; constantly

  副词，表示动作持续或者状态持续不变。

  This is an adverb indicating an unchanged action or state.

  > (1) 计划生育政策自从1980年开始实施以来一直受到官方的称赞，说该政策遏制了人口大规模增长。
  >
  > (2) 一直关注中国计划生育政策的英国人口老龄化学会学者皮尔·波特认为，近40年的计划生育政策可以说是中国人口战略史上的成功一步。
  >
  > (3) 他上大学已经三年了，可还是一直保持跟中学老师的联系。
  >
  > (4) 我一直喜欢看京剧，最近又喜欢上了昆曲。

- **一旦** once; in case; now that

  不确定的时间词，表示有一天。"一旦……就……"用于一个假设的情形，用法接近"如果/要是……就……"。

  "一旦" is a temporal word for an uncertain time, meaning "once" or "one day in the future…" The phrase is used in an assumed situation. The usage is close to that of "如果/要是……就……"

  > (1) 一旦中国进入老龄化发展阶段，就会在国际上越来越缺少竞争力。
  >
  > (2) 夫妻二人一旦失去相互的信任，就很难重新建立信任感。
  >
  > (3) 开车要时时注意安全。一旦大意，就会出事故。
  >
  > (4) 这个房子已经长年失修，一旦发生轻微地震，就会倒塌。

- **导致** to lead to; to bring about; to result in; to cause; to give rise to

动词：引起，书面语；造成（常用于不好的结果）：导致失明、导致犯罪等。

This is a verb that means "to lead, cause, or bring about" and is a written expression. It is often used for negative consequences, such as to cause blindness, lead to criminal behavior, etc.

(1) 现有人口政策会导致城乡人口发展不均衡的现象加重。
(2) 上个世纪50年代中国没有采用马寅初的人口控制政策，导致了人口膨胀。
(3) 2008年的金融危机导致了全球的经济下滑。
(4) 城乡经济发展的不平衡容易导致严重的城乡差别和两极分化。

- **一向** consistently; all along; lately

副词，有两个用法。1) 向来，从来（例1、3、4）；2) 表示行为、情况从上次到现在的一段时间（例2和例5）。

This is an adverb that has two usages: 1) "always, all along" (see examples 1, 3, and 4); 2) "from the last time one did something or was in a certain state up until now" (see examples 2 and 5).

(1) 家庭养老一向是中国人传统的养老模式。
(2) 她一向住在纽约。
(3) 我一向都是早睡早起。
(4) 小李一向吃素。
(5) 你一向可好？

> 副课文 *Supplementary Text*

云南"光棍村"：人口性别比例失衡一案

近年来，农村适龄男女比例严重失调，大龄男青年娶妻难的问题令人担忧。以宣威市文兴乡赵家村为例，该村30岁以上还没有娶妻成家的男青年就达40多人。是什么造成这样的状况呢？记者作了进一步了解。

贫困是娶妻难的主因

该村共有农户105户480人，人均纯收入仅1000余元。这个村子里的女青年大多不愿意嫁在本村，有的早早嫁到外村，有的长期外出打工后远嫁他乡。而外村的女青年也不愿意嫁到这个村，致使村中的男青年只能打"光棍"。对他们而言，娶妻、生子成了一种奢望，长期下来，性格变得孤僻和怪异，自身生理、心理、精神压力极大，其家庭也受到影响。近几年来，这个村的男青年很少有娶到媳妇成家的。据统计部门数字显示，自2000年全国第五次人口普查以来，该村人口一直呈现负增长状态。

农村许多男青年娶不上媳妇，不仅影响到这些人及其家庭的生活，也直接关系到农村经济的进一步发展和社会的和谐稳定。

男女性别歧视酿"苦果"

长期以来，在广大农村，特别是边远贫穷落后的山区，由于受"重男轻女""传宗接代""养儿防老"等传统观念的影响，一些农民非法实施胎儿性别鉴定和选择性别的人工妊娠行为；有的家庭即使生了女孩，也会忍痛送人领养；有人甚至违反人口与计划生育政策，强行超生，不生男孩誓不罢休。种种结果导致农村出生人口男女性别比例偏高甚至失衡，最直接的结果便是众多大龄男青年的出现。

此外，一些贫困农村劳动力大量流入城市或发达地区，家中只剩老人、儿童及部分已婚妇女，适龄的女青年少，造成一大批农村大龄男青年难以成家。

"男盈女亏时代"已经来临

中国社会科学院发布的2010年《社会蓝皮书》指出,目前中国19岁以下年龄段的人口性别比严重失衡,到2020年,中国处于婚龄的男性人数将比女性多出2400万。经测算,届时将有上千万适龄男性面临"娶妻难"。有人说,这折射出"男盈女亏"的时代已经来临。南开大学经济学院人口与发展研究所教授原新说:"在短短二十多年的时间里,出生人口性别比偏高地区从东部向西部,从农村向城市迅速蔓延,几乎覆盖全国各地。"

专家忧虑地指出:家庭是社会的基础,家庭的稳定是社会稳定的前提。当婚而不能婚的男性剧增,会危及婚姻和家庭稳定,大大增加买卖婚姻、拐卖妇女、卖淫嫖娼等违法犯罪行为。男女比例失调还会带来就业挤压问题。男性劳动力过剩会增加劳动力就业市场的竞争,加剧女性就业难度;某些行业和职业中,可能出现女性短缺而要男性替代的现象。出生人口性别比失衡已成为中国社会一大"顽疾",需要引起政府和社会的高度重视。

讨论题 Discussion

根据课文内容回答下列问题

(Please answer the following questions based on the text)

1. 什么是"光棍"和"打光棍"?为什么赵家村叫"光棍村"?
2. 为什么女青年不愿意嫁到赵家村?打光棍对赵家村的男青年有什么不好的影响?对家庭和社会有什么影响?
3. 造成赵家村男女性别比例失衡,大龄男青年偏多的主要原因有哪些?
4. 男女比例失调在中国是个别现象还是普遍现象?这个问题会带来什么社会隐患?中国应该怎么解决这个问题?
5. 美国有没有男女比例失衡的问题?为什么?

生词 New Words

1	光棍		guānggùn	n.	bachelor, unmarried man
2	失衡		shīhéng	v.	to lose balance
3	适龄	適齡	shìlíng	n.	of the right age
4	失调	失調	shī tiáo	v.o.	to lose balance
5	大龄	大齡	dàlíng	n.	above the average age for marriage
6	娶		qǔ	v.	to marry (a woman)
7	妻		qī	n./b.f.	wife
8	主因		zhǔyīn	n.	major cause, main reason
9	农户	農戶	nónghù	n.	peasant household
10	纯	純	chún	adj.	pure, net
11	余	餘	yú	num.	more than, surplus
12	村子		cūnzi	n.	village
13	外出		wàichū	v.	to go out, to go out of town on business
14	打工		dǎ gōng	v.o.	to have a temporary job, to do part time job
15	他乡	他鄉	tāxiāng	n.	a place far away from home, an alien land
16	致使		zhìshǐ	v.	to cause, to lead to, to result in
17	奢望		shēwàng	n./v.	extravagant hopes, wild wishes; to aim high
18	孤僻		gūpì	adj.	unsociable and eccentric, solitary
19	怪异	怪異	guàiyì	adj.	weird, bizarre, strange
20	媳妇	媳婦	xífù	n.	wife, son's wife, daughter-in-law
21	普查		pǔchá	v./n.	to census; general survey
22	呈现	呈現	chéngxiàn	v.	to appear, to present, to display
23	负	負	fù	adj.	minus, negative

24	和谐	和諧	héxié	adj.	harmonious
25	男女		nánnǚ	n.	men and women, male-female
26	酿	釀	niàng	v./b.f.	to make (wine); to lead to, to result in
27	苦果		kǔguǒ	n.	bitter pill, painful result
28	边远	邊遠	biānyuǎn	adj.	far from the center, remote, outlying
29	贫穷	貧窮	pínqióng	adj.	poor, needy, impoverished
30	传宗接代	傳宗接代	chuánzōng-jiēdài	f.e.	to continue one's family line
31	非法		fēifǎ	adj.	illegal, unlawful, illicit
32	鉴定	鑒定	jiàndìng	v.	to appraise, to identify, to authenticate
33	忍痛		rěn tòng	v.o.	(oft. unwillingly) to bear and suffer pain
34	领养	領養	lǐngyǎng	v.	to adopt (a child)
35	强行	強行	qiángxíng	v.	to force, to do sth. using coercive methods
36	超生		chāoshēng	v.	to have children outside the state plan
37	誓不罢休	誓不罷休	shìbúbàxiū	f.e.	to swear not to give up
38	流入		liúrù	v.	to flow into, to drift into, to influx
39	盈		yíng	v./adj.	to be filled with, to be full of; to have a surplus of
40	亏	虧	kuī	v.	to be short of, to lose, to have a deficit
41	届时	屆時	jièshí	adv.	at the appointed time, on the occasion, at the scheduled time
42	折射		zhéshè	v./n.	to reflect; reflection
43	经济学院	經濟學院	jīngjì xuéyuàn	n.p.	school of economics
44	人口与发展研究所	人口與發展研究所	rénkǒu yǔ fāzhǎn yánjiūsuǒ	n.p.	institute for population and development
45	蔓延	蔓延	mànyán	v.	to extend, to creep, to spread
46	覆盖	覆蓋	fùgài	v.	to cover, to overlap

47	基础	基礎	jīchǔ	n.	foundation, base
48	前提		qiántí	n.	premise, prerequisite
49	剧增	劇增	jùzēng	v.	to leap, to surge, to soar
50	危及		wēijí	v.	to endanger, to threat, to imperil
51	拐卖	拐賣	guǎimài	v.	to abduct and traffic people, to kidnap and sell
52	卖淫	賣淫	mài yín	v.o.	to prostitute oneself, to whore
53	嫖娼		piáo chāng	v.o.	to go whoring, to go to prostitutes
54	挤压	擠壓	jǐyā	v.	to crimp, to squeeze, to press
55	过剩		guòshèng	v.	to excess, to surplus, to everplus
56	加剧	加劇	jiājù	v.	to exacerbate, to embitter, to accelerate
57	短缺		duǎnquē	v.	to be short of, to be in short supply
58	顽疾	頑疾	wánjí	n.	chronic disease, recurring illness

专有名词 Proper nouns

1	云南	雲南	Yúnnán	Yunnan Province
2	宣威市		Xuānwēi Shì	Xuanwei City in Yunnan Province
3	文兴乡	文興鄉	Wénxīng Xiāng	Wenxing County
4	赵家村	趙家村	Zhàojiā Cūn	Zhao Village
5	中国社会科学院	中國社會科學院	Zhōngguó Shèhuì Kēxuéyuàn	Chinese Academy of Social Sciences (CASS)
6	社会蓝皮书	社會藍皮書	Shèhuì Lánpíshū	Social Blue Book
7	南开大学	南開大學	Nánkāi Dàxué	Nankai University
8	原新		Yuán Xīn	*a person's name*

# 生词索引

主课文部分

A

艾滋病		àizībìng	n.	AIDS	2
盎然		àngrán	adj.	abundant, full	4

B

把握		bǎwò	v./n.	to grasp, to seize; certainty of success	1
磅		bàng	n./m(n)	pound	7
褒贬	褒貶	bāobiǎn	v.	to appraise, to judge	8
爆发	爆發	bàofā	v.	to erupt, to break out	1
悲观	悲觀	bēiguān	adj.	pessimistic	8
背道而驰	背道而馳	bèidào-érchí	f.e	to go in the opposite direction	6
本人		běnrén	pron.	oneself, I (me, myself); in person	7
壁垒	壁壘	bìlěi	n.	barrier	1
变革	變革	biàngé	v.	to transform, to reform, to change	4
便捷		biànjié	adj.	direct and simple, convenient, easy	3
并发症	併發症	bìngfāzhèng	n.	complication	6
剥夺	剝奪	bōduó	v.	to deprive, to expropriate, to strip (of)	5
不顾	不顧	búgù	v.	to disregard, to ignore	6
不仅仅	不僅僅	bùjǐnjǐn	conj.	not only	8
不可		bùkě	aux.	should not, must not	8
不满	不滿	bùmǎn	adj.	resentful, discontented, dissatisfied	6
不惜		bùxī	v.	not stint, not spare, at all costs	5
不屑一顾	不屑一顧	búxièyígù	f.e.	not worth a glance	2
不懈		búxiè	adj.	untiring, unremitting, indefatigable	5
不休		bùxiū	adv.	endlessly, ceaselessly	6
不已		bùyǐ	v.	to be endless, endlessly, incessantly	3
不止		bùzhǐ	v.	to be more than, to exceed, not limited to	7
不至于	不至於	búzhìyú	adv.	cannot go so far, be unlikely	2
步伐		bùfá	n.	pace, (measured) step	3

C

猜测	猜測	cāicè	v.	to guess, to conjecture, to surmise	8
材		cái	n.	material	3
裁定		cáidìng	v.	to rule, to judge, to adjudicate	2
裁决	裁決	cáijué	v.	to judge, to adjudicate	2
采纳	採納	cǎinà	v.	to accept, to adopt	3
参议员	參議員	cānyìyuán	n.	senator	4
残疾	殘疾	cánjí	n.	disability, handicap	3
残酷	殘酷	cánkù	adj.	cruel, brutal, ruthless	2
操守		cāoshǒu	n.	work ethic, personal integrity	7
产能	產能	chǎnnéng	n.	capacity of production	1
产物	產物	chǎnwù	n.	outcome, result (of), product	4
常年		chángnián	n./adv.	throughout the year, all the year round	4
超越		chāoyuè	v.	to surpass, to transcend, to go beyond	4
巢		cháo	n.	nest of a bird, nest, beehive	8
成语	成語	chéngyǔ	n.	idiom	2
诚信	誠信	chéngxìn	n.	sincerity and honesty	7
城乡	城鄉	chéngxiāng	n.	city and countryside, urban and rural	8
城镇	城鎮	chéngzhèn	n.	cities and towns	1
乘坐		chéngzuò	v.	to ride (in a vehicle), to embark	7
崇尚		chóngshàng	v.	to uphold, to advocate	2
丑闻	醜聞	chǒuwén	n.	scandal	5
出世		chūshì	v.	to be born, to come into the world	6
传单	傳單	chuándān	n.	leaflet, handbill, flyer	6
传导	傳導	chuándǎo	v.	to transmit, to conduct	4
戳穿		chuōchuān	v.	to pierce through, to expose, to reveal	7
此前		cǐqián	n.	prior to a given time or event	5
刺激		cìjī	n./v.	stimulation, stimulus; to provoke, to excite	1
粗略		cūlüè	adv.	roughly, approximately	8
催生		cuīshēng	v.	to expedite delivery	1
存储	存儲	cúnchǔ	v.	to store, to keep	3
存放		cúnfàng	v.	to store, to leave with	5

D

简体	繁体	拼音	词类	英文	课
打印		dǎyìn	v.	to print	3
大本营	大本營	dàběnyíng	n.	headquarter, base camp	6
大逆不道		dànì-búdào	f.e.	to commit high treason	2
大同小异	大同小異	dàtóngxiǎoyì	f.e.	much the same with only minor differences	8
大致		dàzhì	adv.	approximately, roughly, in general	2
逮捕		dàibǔ	v.	to arrest	6
代码	代碼	dàimǎ	n.	code	4
代名词	代名詞	dàimíngcí	n.	synonym	2
单纯	單純	dānchún	adj.	simple	1
单独	單獨	dāndú	adv./attr	alone, solely, by oneself; here it is an abbreviation, meaning "one side of the married couple is a single child".	8
当中	當中	dāngzhōng	n.	among	3
得出		déchū	v(c)	to reach (a conclusion), to obtain (a result)	8
得益		déyì	v.	to receive benefit, to benefit, to profit	4
灯具	燈具	dēngjù	n.	lamp	3
低级	低級	dījí	adj.	low level, elementary, vulgar	7
颠覆	顛覆	diānfù	v.	to overturn, to overthrow	4
典故		diǎngù	n.	classic allusion, literary quotation	2
电路	電路	diànlù	n.	(electric) circuit	4
电子学	電子學	diànzǐxué	n.	electronics	4
顶级	頂級	dǐngjí	n.	top level	4
动画片	動畫片	dònghuàpiàn	n.	animated cartoon, animated film	5
动力	動力	dònglì	n.	motivation, drive, driving force	4
斗	鬥	dòu	v.	to fight, to tussle	5
读物	讀物	dúwù	n.	reading material	2
对外	對外	duì wài	v.o.	external, foreign	1
堕胎	墮胎	duò tāi	v.o.	abortion; to abort	6

E

简体	繁体	拼音	词类	英文	课
恶劣	惡劣	èliè	adj.	bad, despicable, nasty	6
遏制		èzhì	v.	to restrain, to control	1
儿童	兒童	értóng	n.	children	8
二氧化碳		èryǎnghuàtàn	n.	carbon dioxide	1

F

发放	發放	fāfàng	v.	to send out, to give out, to provide	6
发起	發起	fāqǐ	v.	to initiate, to start, to launch	6
罚	罰	fá	v.	to punish, to penalize, to discipline	5
范畴	範疇	fànchóu	n.	category, domain, scope	2
访	訪	fǎng	b.f.	visit, call on	2
访谈	訪談	fǎngtán	v.	to interview	2
飞人	飛人	fēirén	n.	flying man, fast runner	5
废止	廢止	fèizhǐ	v.	to abolish, to annul, to put an end to	6
夫妇	夫婦	fūfù	n.	husband and wife, married couple	3
夫妻		fūqī	n.	husband and wife, spouse	8
肤色	膚色	fūsè	n.	color of skin	4
服用		fúyòng	v.	to take (medicine)	5
浮华	浮華	fúhuá	adj.	flashy, ostentatious, flamboyant	4
符合		fúhé	v.	to accord with, to tally with	8
父辈	父輩	fùbèi	n.	elder generation	8
复苏	復蘇	fùsū	v.	to resuscitate	1
复制	複製	fùzhì	v.	to duplicate, to reproduce	3
富有		fùyǒu	v./adj.	to be full of; wealthy, rich	6

G

感慨		gǎnkǎi	v./n.	to sigh with emotion; emotional lament	2
感染		gǎnrǎn	v.	to infect	3
钢铁	鋼鐵	gāngtiě	n.	iron and steel	1
高等		gāoděng	attr.	higher, advanced, high-level	4
高高在上		gāogāo-zàishàng	f.e.	be far from the masses and reality, be high above	3
高速		gāosù	attr.	high speed, super-speed	1
高位		gāowèi	n.	high position or post	7
各国	各國	gèguó	n.	each country, every country	5
跟随	跟隨	gēnsuí	v.	to follow, to go after	5
更新		gēngxīn	v.	to renew, to replace, to update	5
公平		gōngpíng	adj.	fair, just, impartial	5
公投		gōngtóu	n.	referendum	6
共生		gòngshēng	v.	to grow together; intergrowth, to paragenesis, symbiosis	5
构	構	gòu	b.f.	to construct, to form, to build	4

估算		gūsuàn	v.	to rough estimate, to reckon	8
孤单	孤單	gūdān	adj.	lonely, friendless, alone	8
刮目相看		guāmù-xiāngkàn	f.e.	to treat a person with increased respect, to look at a person with new eyes	4
关爱	關愛	guān'ài	v.	to express solicitude for the well being of, to concern and love	8
惯	慣	guàn	v.	to be used to, to be accustomed to	7
光彩		guāngcǎi	n.	luster, splendor, glory	7
光环	光環	guānghuán	n.	aura, glory, ring of light	7
规避	規避	guībì	v.	to evade, to dodge, to elude	8
硅胶	硅膠	guījiāo	n.	silica gel	3
国防	國防	guófáng	n.	national defense	3
国民	國民	guómín	n.	people of a nation	1
过剩	過剩	guòshèng	v.	to excess, to overabundance, to surplus	1

H

还原	還原	huán yuán	v.o.	to return to the original condition/shape	3
海啸	海嘯	hǎixiào	n.	tsunami, tidal wave	1
悍然		hànrán	adv.	outrageously, brazenly, flagrantly	6
行走		xíngzǒu	v.	to walk, to go about	3
航天		hángtiān	n.	aerospace, cosmonautics	3
合法化		héfǎhuà	v.	to legalize, to make legal	6
核实	核實	héshí	v.	to verify, to check	7
后果	後果	hòuguǒ	n.	consequence, aftermath	3
互		hù	adv.	mutually; mutual, each other	8
划时代	劃時代	huàshídài	adj.	epoch making	6
华语	華語	Huáyǔ	n.	Chinese language	2
化验	化驗	huàyàn	v.	to do laboratory test	5
话语	話語	huàyǔ	n.	speech, utterance	7
怀孕	懷孕	huái yùn	v.o.	to be pregnant, to conceive	6
谎话	謊話	huǎnghuà	n.	lie, falsehood	7
谎言	謊言	huǎngyán	n.	lie, falsehood	7
辉煌	輝煌	huīhuáng	adj.	brilliant, splendid, glorious	7
回到		huídào	v(c)	to return to, to go back to	4
回顾	回顧	huígù	v.	to review, to retrospect, to look back	7
婚礼	婚禮	hūnlǐ	n.	wedding ceremony, wedding	3
婚纱	婚紗	hūnshā	n.	wedding dress, bridal veil	3

混合		hùnhé	v.	to mix, to blend, to mingle	4
火箭弹	火箭彈	huǒjiàndàn	n.	rocket, missile	7
或是		huòshì	conj.	or, perhaps	6

J

机遇	機遇	jīyù	n.	opportunity	1
机组	機組	jīzǔ	n.	flight crew, aircrew	7
基金会	基金會	jījīnhuì	n.	foundation, board of directors of a fund	4
基于	基於	jīyú	prep.	because of, in view of, based on	2
畸形		jīxíng	adj.	deformity, malformation, abnormal	3
给予	給予	jǐyǔ	v.	to give, to render, to offer	7
计	計	jì	v.	to calculate, to count	8
计生	計生	jìshēng	abbr.	family planning (about having children)	8
记载	記載	jìzǎi	v./n.	to record; record	2
伎俩	伎俩	jìliǎng	n.	trick, maneuver, illicit means	7
纪录	紀錄	jìlù	n.	record	5
加深		jiāshēn	v.	to deepen	2
加重		jiāzhòng	v.	to make or become heavier	8
假肢		jiǎzhī	n.	artificial limb	3
坚守	堅守	jiānshǒu	v.	to stick to, to hold fast to, to stand fast	6
坚信	堅信	jiānxìn	v.	to firmly believe	4
监禁	監禁	jiānjìn	v.	to take into custody, to imprison	6
煎饼	煎餅	jiānbing	n.	pancake	3
检测	檢測	jiǎncè	v.	to check, to test, to examine	5
检察官	檢察官	jiǎncháguān	n.	public prosecutor	6
检验	檢驗	jiǎnyàn	v./n.	to test, to examine, to inspect; examination	4
见解	見解	jiànjiě	n.	view, opinion	4
奖金	獎金	jiǎngjīn	n.	bonus, prize, premium	5
奖牌	獎牌	jiǎngpái	n.	medal	5
角落		jiǎoluò	n.	corner, remote place	4
脚	腳	jiǎo	n.	foot	3
教练	教練	jiàoliàn	n.	coach	5
接纳	接納	jiēnà	v.	to admit (into an organization), to accept	2
揭示		jiēshì	v.	to reveal, to bring to light	7
截止		jiézhǐ	v(c)	to end, to close	8

戒指		jièzhi	n.	ring	3
界		jiè	b.f.	boundary, border, circles, world	7
金牌		jīnpái	n.	gold medal	7
尽头	盡頭	jìntóu	n.	end, extremity	5
进程	進程	jìnchéng	n.	course, process, progress	1
近代		jìndài	n.	modern times	5
禁忌		jìnjì	n./v.	taboo; to avoid, to abstain from	2
禁赛	禁賽	jìnsài	v.	suspend, to ban (from a specific sports)	5
经济学	經濟學	jīngjìxué	n.	economics	8
精疲力竭		jīngpí-lìjié	adj.	worn out, exhausted	5
精英		jīngyīng	n.	elite	4
竞争力	競爭力	jìngzhēnglì	n.	competitive power or strength	8
九死一生		jiǔsǐ-yìshēng	f.e.	a hairbreadth escape; barely escape	7
酒精		jiǔjīng	n.	alcohol, spirit, ethyl alcohol	5
居		jū	v./b.f.	to reside, to be (in a certain position), to occupy (a place)	7
居民		jūmín	n.	resident, inhabitant	8
居住		jūzhù	v.	to live, to reside, to dwell	6
举措	舉措	jǔcuò	n.	move, act, initiative	1
举例	舉例	jǔ lì	v.o.	to give an example, to sample	8
飓风	颶風	jùfēng	n.	hurricane	7
均衡		jūnhéng	adj.	balanced, even	8

K

开启	開啟	kāiqǐ	v.	to open, to initiate	3
开支	開支	kāizhī	v./n.	to spend, to expend; expenses, expenditure	8
堪		kān	aux.	may, can	3
侃侃而谈	侃侃而談	kǎnkǎn-értán	f.e.	to talk with ease and confidence	4
抗议	抗議	kàngyì	v.	to protest	6
考验	考驗	kǎoyàn	n./v.	test, trial; to put sb. to the test	6
可持续	可持續	kěchíxù	adj.	sustainable	1
可信		kěxìn	adj.	credible, believable, trustworthy	7
课堂	課堂	kètáng	n.	classroom	3
夸大	誇大	kuādà	v.	to exaggerate, to overstate, to magnify	7

L

拉动	拉動	lādòng	v.	to pull, to drive, to promote	1
拉拉		lālā	n.	lesbian	2
来临	來臨	láilín	v.	to arrive, to come, to approach	3
栏目	欄目	lánmù	n.	heading or title of a column in a newspaper or magazine, etc.	2
老兵		lǎobīng	n.	veterans, veteran soldiers	7
老龄	老齡	lǎolíng	n.	aging, elderly people, old age	8
老年		lǎonián	n.	old age, elderly, aging	8
老鼠		lǎoshǔ	n.	mouse, rat	3
乐于	樂於	lèyú	v.	to be happy to, to take delight in	7
冷淡		lěngdàn	adj.	cold, indifferent	8
力图	力圖	lìtú	v.	to try hard to, strive to do one's best to	4
历	歷	lì	b.f.	to go through, to undergo, to experience	7
联盟	聯盟	liánméng	n.	league, union, coalition	5
亮相		liàng xiàng	v.o.	to strike a pose on stage, to debut	3
留言		liúyán	v.o./n.	to leave comments; message	2
流程		liúchéng	n.	manufacturing, technological process	3
流失		liúshī	v.	to run off, to be washed away, to flow away	7
乱伦	亂倫	luànlún	v.	to be incestuous, to commit incest	6
论题	論題	lùntí	n.	topic	6
螺丝	螺絲	luósī	n.	screw	3

M

麻疹	痲疹	mázhěn	n.	measles, rubeola	6
马拉松	馬拉松	mǎlāsōng	n.	marathon	5
迈进	邁進	màijìn	v(c)	to stride forward, to forge ahead	4
贸易保护主义	貿易保護主義	màoyì bǎohùzhǔyì	n.p.	trade protectionism	1
枚		méi	m(n)	measure word for coins, needle, small objects	5
媒		méi	b.f.	media	1
免费	免費	miǎnfèi	v.o.	to be free of charge	4
面糊	麵糊	miànhù	n.	flour paste	3
面具		miànjù	n.	mask	2
面子		miànzi	n.	reputation, prestige, face	2
民调	民調	míndiào	n.	opinion poll	6

民营	民營	mínyíng	attr.	privately run (of enterprises), nongovernmental business	1
名人		míngrén	n.	celebrity, famous person	7
名义	名義	míngyì	n.	in the name of	2
明明		míngmíng	adv.	obviously, plainly, undoubtedly	6
明智		míngzhì	adj.	sagacious, wise, sensible	8
模式		móshì	n.	model, pattern, mode	1
慕课	慕課	mùkè	n.	Mooc, Massive Open Online Course	4

N

内需	內需	nèixū	n.	domestic market demand	1
尿		niào	n./v.	urine; to urinate	5
农场	農場	nóngchǎng	n.	farm, ranch, homestead	8

P

蹒跚	蹣跚	pánshān	v.	to dodder, to stagger, to stumble	3
判		pàn	v./b.f.	to sentence, to judge	2
判处	判處	pànchǔ	v.	to sentence, to condemn, to penalize	6
培训	培訓	péixùn	v.	to train	8
配套		pèi tào	v.o.	to match, to form a complete set	3
披露		pīlù	v.	to reveal, to disclose, to publish, to announce	7
偏见	偏見	piānjiàn	n.	prejudice, bias	2
偏远	偏遠	piānyuǎn	adj.	remote, faraway	4
骗子	騙子	piànzi	n.	cheater, liar, swindler	5
漂		piāo	v.	to drift, to float about	7
贫富	貧富	pínfù	n.	the poor and the rich	4
频道	頻道	píndào	n.	channel, frequency channel	2
品		pǐn	b.f.	article, product	3
平衡		pínghéng	n./v.	balance, equilibrium; to counterpoise	1
平民		píngmín	n.	ordinary people, civilian	4
平添		píngtiān	v.	to add sth. unexpectedly	7
平息		píngxī	v.	to quiet down, to subside, to suppress	7
评价	評價	píngjià	v./n.	to appraise, to evaluate; evaluation	2
凭借	憑藉	píngjiè	v.	to depend on, by means of	4

颇	頗	pō	adv.	quite, very, considerably	6
迫害		pòhài	v.	to persecute, to torture	2
迫降		pòjiàng	v.	to have a forced landing, to have an emergency landing	7
破获	破獲	pòhuò	v.	to crack a case and capture the criminal, to uncover (a criminal plot)	3
普及		pǔjí	v.	to popularize, to disseminate, to spread	3

Q

歧视	歧視	qíshì	v./n.	to discriminate against, to treat with bias; discrimination (against someone)	2
旗		qí	n.	flag, banner	4
器		qì	b.f.	instrument, apparatus, weapon	5
千千万万	千千萬萬	qiānqiān-wànwàn	r.f.	thousands upon thousands	4
签署	簽署	qiānshǔ	v.	to sign officially, to subscribe	6
前往		qiánwǎng	v.	to go, to leave for, to proceed to	6
前线	前線	qiánxiàn	n.	front, frontline, battlefront	7
前沿		qiányán	n.	cutting-edge, frontline, front edge	3
谴责	譴責	qiǎnzé	v.	to condemn, to denounce, to criticize	6
强奸	強姦	qiángjiān	v.	to rape, to assault sexually	6
悄然		qiǎorán	adv.	quietly, softly, noiselessly	3
切除		qiēchú	v.	to resect, to cut off	3
亲	親	qīn	b.f.	in person, personally	7
清算		qīngsuàn	v.	to carefully calculate and check, to expose and criticize all evil-doings or mistakes, and inflict punishment	6
求助		qiúzhù	v.	to seek help, to ask sb. for help	2
驱使	驅使	qūshǐ	v.	to drive, to propel, to prompt	5
趋势	趨勢	qūshì	n.	trend, current, tendency	1
取胜	取勝	qǔshèng	v.	to win, to succeed	1
取向		qǔxiàng	n.	orientation	8
权威	權威	quánwēi	n.	authority, power and prestige	2
全民		quánmín	n.	nation-wide, all the people, the entire people	6
全球		quánqiú	n.	whole world	1

R

热线	熱線	rèxiàn	n.	hotline (communications link)	2

人口		rénkǒu	n.	population	8
认定	認定	rèndìng	v.	firmly believe, to affirm	6
仍旧	仍舊	réngjiù	adv.	to still, yet	5
日前		rìqián	n.	a few days ago, the other day	3
荣耀	榮耀	róngyào	n.	honor, glory	5
荣誉	榮譽	róngyù	n.	honor, glory, credit	7
容器		róngqì	n.	container, receptacle, vessel	3
融合		rónghé	v.	to mix together, to fuse; assimilation, fusion	3
融入		róngrù	v.	to merge into, to integrate into	1
柔软	柔軟	róuruǎn	adj.	soft	3
如日中天		rúrì-zhōngtiān	f.e.	at the apex of one's power or career	7
入学	入學	rù xué	v.o.	to enroll in a school or college	4
软骨	軟骨	ruǎngǔ	n.	cartilage	3
弱势	弱勢	ruòshì	adj.	weak, vulnerable	6

S

赛跑	賽跑	sàipǎo	v.	to race	1
扇		shàn	m(n)	measure word for doors or windows	3
赡养	贍養	shànyǎng	v.	to support, to provide for	8
上半年		shàngbànnián	n.	first half of a year	1
上台	上臺	shàng tái	v.o.	to appear on the stage, to come (or rise) to power, to assume power	6
设施	設施	shèshī	n.	installation, facilities	4
设置	設置	shèzhì	v./n.	to set up, to install; sets, settings	1
深度		shēndù	n./adj.	depth; in depth	4
审查	審查	shěnchá	v.	to examine, to inspect, to investigate	6
慎		shèn	b.f./n.	careful, cautious	6
升值	昇值	shēngzhí	v.	to rise in value	1
生平		shēngpíng	n.	ever since one's birth; one's entire life	3
生育		shēngyù	v.	to give birth to	2
声誉	聲譽	shēngyù	n.	reputation, fame, prestige	7
尸检	屍檢	shījiǎn	v.	autopsy	5
尸体	屍體	shītǐ	n.	dead body, corpse, remains	7

失望		shīwàng	adj.	disappointed	8
失职	失職	shī zhí	v.o.	to neglect one's duty, dereliction of duty	7
诗歌	詩歌	shīgē	n.	poems and songs, poetry	4
实物	實物	shíwù	n.	material object	3
实验室	實驗室	shíyànshì	n.	laboratory	5
食品		shípǐn	n.	food, foodstuff	8
史		shǐ	b.f./n.	history	5
市政厅	市政廳	shìzhèngtīng	n.	city hall	2
视	視	shì	b.f.	to look at, to regard	6
视频	視頻	shìpín	n.	video clips	4
视网膜	視網膜	shìwǎngmó	n.	retinal	3
首饰	首飾	shǒushì	n.	jewelry	3
首席		shǒuxí	n.	chief	4
受罚	受罰	shòu fá	v.o.	to be punished, to receive punishment	7
受益		shòuyì	v.	to profit by, to benefit from	4
授课	授課	shòu kè	v.o.	to give lessons, to give instruction	4
书面	書面	shūmiàn	n.	written, in written form, in writing	6
数目	數目	shùmù	n.	number, amount	8
率先		shuàixiān	v.	to take the lead, to be the first to do sth.	2
双性恋	雙性戀	shuāngxìngliàn	n.	bisexuality	2
水涨船高	水漲船高	shuǐzhǎng chuángāo	f.e.	particulars improve as general situation does; all ships rise with the tide	8
说谎	說謊	shuō huǎng	v.o.	to tell a lie, to lie	7
司法官		sīfǎguān	n.	judiciary, law officer	2
死板		sǐbǎn	adj.	rigid, inflexible, stiff	4
死刑		sǐxíng	n.	death penalty	2
塑		sù	v.	to model, to mould	8
塑像		sùxiàng	n.	statue	3
随地	隨地	suídì	adv.	anywhere, in any place	4
随后	隨後	suíhòu	adv.	soon afterward, subsequently, then	7

T

他人		tārén	pr.	others, other people, other person	2
胎		tāi	n./m(n)	fetus, embryo, baby	8
胎儿	胎兒	tāi'ér	n.	fetus, embryo	6
抬头	抬頭	tái tóu	v.o.	to gain ground, to rise	1

态势	態勢	tàishì	n.	state, stance, posture	1
探求		tànqiú	v.	to pursue, to search for, to seek	1
探讨	探討	tàntǎo	v.	to inquire into, to discuss, to probe	4
特征	特徵	tèzhēng	n.	characteristic, feature, property	8
特质	特質	tèzhì	n.	special quality, characteristics	4
疼痛		téngtòng	adj.	ache, painful	3
腾飞	騰飛	téngfēi	v.	to fly swiftly upward, to soar	3
提交		tíjiāo	v.	to submit, to refer to	4
提升	提昇	tíshēng	v./n.	to promote, to upgrade, to elevate	1
题材	題材	tícái	n.	subject matter, theme	2
体能	體能	tǐnéng	n.	stamina, physical ability, fitness	5
体坛	體壇	tǐtán	n.	sports circles, the sporting world	5
替代		tìdài	v.	to substitute for, to replace; substitution	3
添丁		tiān dīng	v.o.	to have a baby born into the family	8
田径运动员	田徑運動員	tiánjìng yùndòngyuán	n.p.	track and field athletes	5
条例	條例	tiáolì	n.	regulations, rules, ordinances	5
条文	條文	tiáowén	n.	article, clause	2
调整	調整	tiáozhěng	v.	to adjust, to tinker up	8
停职	停職	tíng zhí	v.o.	to suspend sb. from his duties	7
通往		tōngwǎng	v.	to lead to	3
同性		tóngxìng	attr.	the same sex, homosexual	2
同性恋	同性戀	tóngxìngliàn	n.	homosexuality	2
头顶	頭頂	tóudǐng	n.	the top of the head	7
头衔	頭銜	tóuxián	n.	official title, academic rank or title	5
透明		tòumíng	adj.	transparent	1
途		tú	b.f.	way, path, route	5
涂脂抹粉	塗脂抹粉	túzhī-mǒfěn	f.e.	to apply facial makeup, to prettify	7
土木工程		tǔmù gōngchéng	n.p.	civil engineering	3
推出		tuīchū	v(c)	to present to the public, to release	3
推进	推進	tuījìn	v.	to advance, to push on, to carry forward	6
褪		tuì	v.	to take off, to shed, to slip out of sth.	4

外界		wàijiè	n.	outside, the outside world, external	7

外衣		wàiyī	n.	coat, outer garment	4
完善		wánshàn	v./adj.	to perfect, to improve; perfect	4
玩具		wánjù	n.	toy, plaything	8
晚间	晚間	wǎnjiān	n.	evening, night	7
晚间新闻	晚間新聞	wǎnjiān xīnwén	n.p.	evening news	7
晚期		wǎnqī	n.	later period, late stage	6
威士忌		wēishìjì	n.	whisky, whiskey	5
违	違	wéi	b.f.	to disobey, to violate	6
违法	違法	wéi fǎ	v.o.	to break the law, to be illegal	6
违禁	違禁	wéijìn	attr./v.	banned, prohibited; to violate a ban	5
温和	溫和	wēnhé	adj.	gentle, mild	2
稳步	穩步	wěnbù	adv.	with steady steps, steadily	1
卧病	臥病	wòbìng	v.	to be sick abed	4
无关	無關	wúguān	v.	to have nothing to do with, to be irrelevant	2
无所不能	無所不能	wúsuǒbùnéng	f.e.	omnipotent, almighty	3
无异	無異	wúyì	v.	to be not different from	6
无助	無助	wúzhù	adj.	helpless	6
误差	誤差	wùchā	n.	error	7

X

析		xī	b.f./v.	to analyze, to dissect	2
席卷	席捲	xíjuǎn	v.	to roll up like a mat, to engulf, to sweep	4
喜糖		xǐtáng	n.	candies or sweets for entertaining friends and relatives at a wedding	3
系列		xìliè	n.	series, set	1
细胞	細胞	xìbāo	n.	cell	3
下滑		xiàhuá	v.	to slide, to decline	1
先天		xiāntiān	n./attr.	congenital, inborn, inherent	3
显	顯	xiǎn	v.	to show, to display, to manifest	3
显而易见	顯而易見	xiǎn'éryìjiàn	f.e.	obviously, evidently, clearly	8
显赫	顯赫	xiǎnhè	adj.	illustrious, celebrated, eminent	7
宪	憲	xiàn	b.f.	constitution, law, statute	6
相对	相對	xiāngduì	adj.	relative, relatively, comparatively	2
相连	相連	xiānglián	v.	to link, to connect	5
相提并论	相提並論	xiāngtí-bìnglùn	f.e.	to mention in the same breath, to place on a par	8
消费	消費	xiāofèi	v.	to consume, to spend	8
萧条	蕭條	xiāotiáo	adj.	(economic) in depression	1

小吃	小喫	xiǎochī	n.	snack, refreshments	3
心疼		xīnténg	v.	to love dearly, to make one's heart ache, to feel sorry	8
新型		xīnxíng	attr.	new type, new pattern	4
薪		xīn	b.f.	salary, wages	7
信任		xìnrèn	v.	to trust, to have confidence in, to believe in	7
兴办	興辦	xīngbàn	v.	to start, to initiate, to set up	4
兴奋剂	興奮劑	xīngfènjì	n.	stimulant, dope, performance enhancement drugs	5
修复	修復	xiūfù	v.	to repair, to restore	3
羞耻	羞恥	xiūchǐ	adj.	sense of shame, ashamed	2
虚假	虛假	xūjiǎ	adj.	false, sham, deceitful	7
需求		xūqiú	n.	demand, need	3
选手	選手	xuǎnshǒu	n.	athlete selected for a sports meet, player, contestant	5
选修	選修	xuǎnxiū	v.	to take as an elective course	2
学府	學府	xuéfǔ	n.	institution of higher learning	4
学者	學者	xuézhě	n.	scholar, literati	4
血管		xuèguǎn	n.	blood vessel, vein, artery	5
血样	血樣	xuèyàng	n.	blood samples	5

Y

压力	壓力	yālì	n.	pressure	2
鸭	鴨	yā	n	duck	3
淹		yān	v./b.f.	to flood, to submerge, to inundate	7
演变	演變	yǎnbiàn	v.	to develop, to evolve	3
厌倦	厭倦	yànjuàn	v.	to be weary of, to be tired of	4
扬言	揚言	yáng yán	v.o.	to threaten	6
仰慕		yǎngmù	v./n.	to admire, to look up to; adoration	7
养老	養老	yǎng lǎo	v.o.	to provide for the aged, to live out one's life in retirement	8
养老金	養老金	yǎnglǎojīn	n.	pension	8
遥不可及	遙不可及	yáobùkějí	f.e.	out of reach	3
药物	藥物	yàowù	n.	medicines, drugs, pharmaceuticals	5
一成不变	一成不變	yìchéngbúbiàn	f.e.	nothing ever changes	8
一向		yíxiàng	adv.	always, all along, the whole time	2
衣袋		yīdài	n.	pocket	5
医疗	醫療	yīliáo	v.	to take medical treatment	1
医药	醫藥	yīyào	n.	medicine	3

依然		yīrán	adv.	still, as before	2
仪式	儀式	yíshì	n.	ceremony, rite, function	2
已然		yǐrán	adv./v.	already; to be already so	8
以便		yǐbiàn	conj.	so that, in order to, so as to	7
异	異	yì	b.f.	different	4
异性恋	異性戀	yìxìngliàn	n.	heterosexuality	2
银幕	銀幕	yínmù	n.	screen	2
引领	引領	yǐnlǐng	v.	to lead	1
隐匿	隱匿	yǐnnì	v.	to conceal, to hide	2
婴儿	嬰兒	yīng'ér	n.	baby, infant	8
永恒		yǒnghéng	adj.	eternal, perpetual	6
勇		yǒng	b.f./n.	courage, bravery	5
用途		yòngtú	n.	use, purpose, application	3
优势	優勢	yōushì	n.	superiority, advantage	1
优异	優異	yōuyì	adj.	excellent, outstanding	4
优越	優越	yōuyuè	adj.	superior, advantageous	4
优质	優質	yōuzhì	adj.	high (or top) quality, high grade	3
犹豫	猶豫	yóuyù	adj.	hesitate, be irresolute, wavering	8
有待		yǒudài	v.	to remain (to be done), to be pending, to await	4
有教无类	有教無類	yǒujiào-wúlèi	f.e.	to provide education to all people without discrimination	4
舆论	輿論	yúlùn	n.	public opinion	2
语	語	yǔ	b.f./v.	language, tongue; to speak	2
预示	預示	yùshì	v.	to forebode, to foreshadow, to betoken	4
愈演愈烈		yùyǎn-yùliè	f.e.	to grow in intensity, to intensify	6
源远流长	源遠流長	yuányuǎn-liúcháng	f.e.	long-standing and well-established, have a long history	2
远远	遠遠	yuǎnyuǎn	r.f.	far away, distant	8
约	約	yuē	adv.	about, approximately	8
孕妇	孕婦	yùnfù	n.	pregnant woman, gravida	6

Z

在场	在場	zàichǎng	v.	to be present, to be on the scene	4
攒	攢	zǎn	v.	to accumulate, to save	1
造假		zào jiǎ	v.o.	to fake, to make fake products	7
增进	增進	zēngjìn	v.	to enhance, to promote	5
增速		zēngsù	n.	growth rate	1

炸弹	炸彈	zhàdàn	n.	bomb, bombshell	7
战场	戰場	zhànchǎng	n.	battlefield, battlefront	7
战地	戰地	zhàndì	n.	battle field	7
战略	戰略	zhànlüè	n.	strategy, tactic	8
着眼	著眼	zhuóyǎn	v.	to have one's eyes on (a goal), to focus on	1
真相		zhēnxiàng	n.	facts, truth	7
斟酌		zhēnzhuó	v.	to consider, to deliberate	8
诊所	診所	zhěnsuǒ	n.	clinic	6
震动	震動	zhèndòng	v.	to shake, to shock, to vibrate	7
镇静	鎮靜	zhènjìng	adj.	sedative, calm, composed	6
争端	爭端	zhēngduān	n.	dispute, controversy, conflict	6
政权	政權	zhèngquán	n.	political power, state power, regime	8
支出		zhīchū	v./n.	to expend; expenses, disbursement	1
直觉	直覺	zhíjué	n.	intuition	2
直升机	直昇機	zhíshēngjī	n.	helicopter, copter	7
值		zhí	v.	to be worth	4
指责	指責	zhǐzé	v.	to blame, to accuse, to find fault with	7
至高无上	至高無上	zhìgāo-wúshàng	f.e.	supreme, sovereign	7
制	製	zhì	v.	to make, to manufacture, to produce	3
制定	製定	zhìdìng	v.	to formulate, to lay down, to draw up	8
制作	製作	zhìzuò	v.	to make, to manufacture to, produce	2
致力		zhì lì	v.o.	to work for, to devote one's efforts to	1
致命		zhìmìng	attr./v.	fatal, mortal, lethal; to cause death	3
智		zhì	b.f./n.	wisdom, intelligence, brainpower	5
终身	終身	zhōngshēn	n.	lifelong, all one's life, lifetime	4
终止	終止	zhōngzhǐ	v.	to stop, to end	5
钟爱	鍾愛	zhōng'ài	v.	to have a passion for, to be very fond of	4
肿瘤	腫瘤	zhǒngliú	n.	tumor	5
种族	種族	zhǒngzú	n.	race (of people)	4
重创	重創	zhòngchuāng	v.	to inflict heavy losses on	1
州长	州長	zhōuzhǎng	n.	governor	6
诸多	諸多	zhūduō	adj.	a good deal, a lot of	4
主播		zhǔbō	n.	anchor (TV)	7
主流		zhǔliú	n.	mainstream	2
主体	主體	zhǔtǐ	n.	centerpiece, main body	1
主义	主義	zhǔyì	n.	systematic doctrine or theory, -ism	6

注射		zhùshè	v.	to inject	5
抓住		zhuāzhù	v(c)	to capture, to catch hold of	5
专程	專程	zhuānchéng	adv.	special trip	6
幢		zhuàng	m(n)	measure word for houses	3
追赶	追趕	zhuīgǎn	v.	to chase after, to pursue	5
追逐		zhuīzhú	v.	to pursue, to chase	5
追踪	追蹤	zhuīzōng	v.	to follow the trail of, to track, to trace	7
资格	資格	zīgé	n.	qualifications	5
子女		zǐnǚ	n.	sons and daughters, offspring	2
自身		zìshēn	n.	self, oneself	4
自习	自習	zìxí	v.	to study by oneself	4
自由主义	自由主義	zìyóu zhǔyì	n.p.	liberalism	6
总值	總值	zǒngzhí	n.	gross or total value	1
纵观	縱觀	zòngguān	v.	to make a comprehensive survey, to take an overall view	1
走路		zǒu lù	v.o.	to walk, to go on foot	3
最高法院		zuìgāo fǎyuàn	n.p.	supreme court	2
作案		zuò àn	v.o.	to commit a crime or an offense	3
作出		zuòchū	v(c)	to make, to work out, to make with	1

副课文部分

A

阿拉伯语	阿拉伯語	Ālābóyǔ	n.	Arabic	4

B

百家争鸣	百家爭鳴	bǎi jiā zhēng míng	f.e.	contention of a hundred schools of thought, to let a hundred schools of thought contend	7
保守		bǎoshǒu	adj.	conservative	2
奔		bèn	v.	to run quickly, to hurry or rush	3
本地		běndì	n.	local	1
边远	邊遠	biānyuǎn	adj.	far from the center, remote, outlying	8
便利		biànlì	adj./v.	convenient, easy; to facilitate	7
拨	撥	bō	v./m(n)	to push aside, to move; group, batch	5

波动	波動	bōdòng	v.	to fluctuate, to rise and fall	5
播放		bōfàng	v.	to broadcast, to transmit, to show	7
博士生		bóshìshēng	n.	doctoral candidate, Ph.d students	7
不明		bùmíng	v./ adj.	to fail to understand, not clear, unknown	7
不容		bùróng	v.	not tolerate, not allow, not brook	6

C

才华	才華	cáihuá	n.	talent, gifts, literary or artistic talent	4
参悟	參悟	cānwù	v.	to realize, to understand from meditation	5
草根		cǎogēn	n.	grass roots	7
策略		cèlüè	n.	tactics, strategy	1
场合	場合	chǎnghé	n.	occasion, situation, conjuncture	4
倡导	倡導	chàngdǎo	v.	to initiate, to propose, to promote	5
超生		chāoshēng	v.	to have children outside the state plan	8
超市		chāoshì	n.	supermarket	1
沉淀	沉澱	chéndiàn	v.	to rest and reflect, to precipitate	5
沉着	沉著	chénzhuó	adj.	composed, calm and collected	5
沉重		chénzhòng	adj.	heavy, serious, critical	6
呈现	呈現	chéngxiàn	v.	to appear, to present, to display	8
承诺	承諾	chéngnuò	v./n.	to agree to do sth.; promise, pledge	1
痴迷	癡迷	chīmí	v.	to be obsessed with, to be addicted to, to be crazy for	5
弛		chí	b.f./adj.	relax, loose	5
出人意料		chūrén-yìliào	f.e.	to exceed all expectations, surprising	4
处事	處事	chǔ shì	v.	to handle affairs, to deal with matters	5
传宗接代	傳宗接代	chuánzōng-jiēdài	f.e.	to continue one's family line	8
创始人	創始人	chuàngshǐrén	n.	founder, originator, creator	4
纯	純	chún	adj.	pure, net	8
词汇	詞彙	cíhuì	n.	vocabulary, lexicon, glossary	4
村子		cūnzi	n.	village	8

D

打工		dǎ gōng	v.o.	to have a temporary job, to do part time job	8
打开	打開	dǎkāi	v(c)	to break open, to undo, to open	3
大出血		dàchūxiě	n.	hematorrhea, heavy bleeding	6
大多		dàduō	adv.	for the most part, many, most	2

大纲	大綱	dàgāng	n.	outline, summary, syllabus	6
大龄	大齡	dàlíng	n.	above the average age for marriage	8
代价	代價	dàijià	n.	price, cost, expense	6
当下	當下	dāngxià	n./adv.	current or present situation; at once, immediately, presently	3
导师	導師	dǎoshī	n.	tutor, teacher, supervisor, mentor	7
到访	到訪	dàofǎng	v.	to come for a visit	4
等候		děnghòu	v.	to wait	2
第一时间	第一時間	dì yī shíjiān	n.p	at the first moment, immediately	7
逗留		dòuliú	v.	to stay, to stop, to linger	3
独树一帜	獨樹一幟	dúshù-yízhì	f.e.	unique; to fly one's own colors	5
堵塞		dǔsè	v.	to stop up, to jam, to block up	1
短缺		duǎnquē	v.	to be short of, to be in short supply	8
段落		duànluò	n.	paragraph	7

E

儿戏	兒戲	érxì	n.	trifling matter; child's play	6

F

发酵	發酵	fājiào	v.	to ferment	7
发泄	發洩	fāxiè	v.	to give vent to, to let off	3
发展中国家	發展中國家	fāzhǎnzhōng guójiā	n.p.	developing country	6
烦恼	煩惱	fánnǎo	adj.	upset, worried, vexed	5
繁荣	繁榮	fánróng	adj.	flourishing, prosperous, booming	3
繁衍		fányǎn	v.	to multiply, to increase gradually in number or quantity	2
反响	反響	fǎnxiǎng	n.	reaction, echo, repercussion	4
放空		fàngkōng	v.	to drift off, to be spaced out	5
非法		fēifǎ	adj.	illegal, unlawful, illicit	8
分析		fēnxī	v./n.	to analyze; analysis	6
风风火火	風風火火	fēngfēng-huǒhuǒ	f.e.	hustling and bustling	5
风险	風險	fēngxiǎn	n.	risk, danger, hazard	6
蜂拥而至	蜂擁而至	fēngyōng-érzhì	f.e.	to stream in	2
负	負	fù	adj.	minus, negative	8
妇科	婦科	fùkē	n.	gynecology	6
附		fù	v.	to add, to attach, to enclose	7
覆盖	覆蓋	fùgài	v.	to cover, to overlap	8

G

敢于	敢於	gǎnyú	v.	to dare to, to have the courage to	4
感悟		gǎnwù	v.	to understand, to be moved and comprehend	5
干果	乾果	gānguǒ	n.	dried fruits	1
高龄	高齡	gāolíng	n.	advanced age, venerable age	7
高中		gāozhōng	n.	high school	4
歌迷		gēmí	n.	fan	2
各抒己见	各抒己見	gè shū jǐ jiàn	f.e.	each expresses his own views	7
根基		gēnjī	n.	foundation, basis	2
根深蒂固		gēnshēn-dìgù	f.e.	deep-rooted, inveterate	2
公布	公佈	gōngbù	v.	to promulgate, to announce, to publish	2
公益		gōngyì	n	public welfare	1
购物	購物	gòu wù	v.o.	to go shopping	1
孤僻		gūpì	adj.	unsociable and eccentric, solitary	8
顾问	顧問	gùwèn	n.	adviser, consultant	4
拐卖	拐賣	guǎimài	v.	to abduct and traffic people, to kidnap and sell	8
怪异	怪異	guàiyì	adj.	weird, bizarre, strange	8
光棍		guānggùn	n.	bachelor, unmarried man	8
广	廣	guǎng	adj.	wide, vast, extensive	7
归功	歸功	guīgōng	v.	to give credit to, to owe to	5
归结	歸結	guījié	v.	to sum up	2
过剩		guòshèng	v.	to excess, to surplus, to everplus	8

H

豪华	豪華	háohuá	adj.	luxurious	1
合格		hégé	adj.	qualified, up to standard	1
和谐	和諧	héxié	adj.	harmonious	8
后代	後代	hòudài	n.	descendants, posterity	2
后期	後期	hòuqī	n.	later stage, later period	2
忽视	忽視	hūshì	v.	to ignore, to neglect, to overlook	6
花甲		huājiǎ	n.	a cycle of sixty years, sixty years of age	3
欢呼	歡呼	huānhū	v.	to cheer, to hail	4
欢笑	歡笑	huānxiào	v.	to laugh heartily	4
患		huàn	v./b.f.	to contract (an illness), to suffer from	6
回头客	回頭客	huítóukè	n.	returned customer	3

| 讳莫如深 | 諱莫如深 | huìmòrúshēn | f.e. | to carefully conceal, to avoid mentioning (scandal), to closely guard a secret | 6 |

J

积压	積壓	jīyā	v.	to keep long in stock, to overstock	1
基础	基礎	jīchǔ	n.	foundation, base	8
急躁		jízào	adj.	irritable, impatient, redheaded	5
挤压	擠壓	jǐyā	v.	to crimp, to squeeze, to press	8
加剧	加劇	jiājù	v.	to exacerbate, to embitter, to accelerate	8
家人		jiārén	n.	family members	7
价位	價位	jiàwèi	n.	price level	1
监管	監管	jiānguǎn	v./n.	to supervise, to keep watch on; supervision	1
监控	監控	jiānkòng	v.	to supervise and control	1
检点	檢點	jiǎndiǎn	v.	to be cautious or restrained	2
简直	簡直	jiǎnzhí	adv.	simply, at all	4
见证	見證	jiànzhèng	v./n.	to witness; testimony	3
剑	劍	jiàn	n.	sword	7
鉴定	鑒定	jiàndìng	v.	to appraise, to identify, to authenticate	8
讲究	講究	jiǎngjiu	v.	to stress, to strive for, to be particular about	5
交谈	交談	jiāotán	v.	to talk, to converse, to chat	4
交往		jiāowǎng	v.	to contact, to date, to be in contact with	6
焦虑	焦慮	jiāolǜ	adj.	worry	3
焦躁		jiāozào	adj.	restless with anxiety, impatient, in a fuss	5
接收		jiēshōu	v.	to receive, to accept	3
接诊	接診	jiēzhěn	v.	to see and treat patients	6
街头巷尾	街頭巷尾	jiētóu-xiàngwěi	f.e.	street corners and alleys, everywhere	7
节奏	節奏	jiézòu	n.	rhythm, pace	3
届时	屆時	jièshí	adv.	at the appointed time, on the occasion, at the scheduled time	8
经管	經管	jīngguǎn	n.	economics and management	4
经济学院	經濟學院	jīngjì xuéyuàn	n.p.	school of economics	8
惊人	驚人	jīngrén	adj.	astonishing, amazing, alarming	7
警方		jǐngfāng	n.	the police	7
竞选	競選	jìngxuǎn	v.	to enter into an election, to campaign, to run for	2
竟然		jìngrán	adv.	unexpectedly, to one's surprise	4
静态	靜態	jìngtài	n.	static state, quiescent condition	5
静心	靜心	jìngxīn	v.	to clear one's mind; meditation	5
久远	久遠	jiǔyuǎn	adj.	far back, ages ago	3

救灾	救災	jiù zāi	v.o.	to provide disaster relief, to send relief to a disaster area	7
剧增	劇增	jùzēng	v.	to leap, to surge, to soar	8
捐款		juān kuǎn	v.o.	to donate money, to contribute funds	7
捐献	捐獻	juānxiàn	v.	to contribute, to donate	1

K

开阔	開闊	kāikuò	adj./v.	wide, broad; to broaden, to widen	5
开设	開設	kāishè	v.	to open (shop)	1
开张	開張	kāi zhāng	v.o.	to open a business	3
抗衡		kànghéng	v.	to compete, to counterweight	2
可谓	可謂	kěwèi	v.	it may be called or said	5
空虚		kōngxū	adj.	hollow, empty	3
苦果		kǔguǒ	n.	bitter pill, painful result	8
苦心		kǔxīn	n.	trouble taken, painstaking efforts	4
狂热	狂熱	kuángrè	adj.	fanatic, fanatical, feverish, mad	3
亏	虧	kuī	v.	to be short of, to lose, to have a deficit	8
扩散	擴散	kuòsàn	v.	to spread, to diffuse, to proliferate	2
扩展	擴展	kuòzhǎn	v.	to expand, to broaden, to spread	2
扩张	擴張	kuòzhāng	v.	to expand, to extend, to enlarge	1

L

拉丁文		Lādīngwén	n.	Latin	4
滥交	濫交	lànjiāo	v./n.	to have a casual sex; promiscuity	2
老外		lǎowài	n.	foreigner (colloquial expression)	4
类似	類似	lèisì	v.	to be analogous, to be similar	3
冷静	冷靜	lěngjìng	adj.	calm, cool-headed	5
历程	歷程	lìchéng	n.	course, process	2
连锁	連鎖	liánsuǒ	adj./attr.	chain, interlocked elements, linkage	1
列举	列舉	lièjǔ	v.	to list	2
零售		língshòu	v.	to retail, to sell retail	1
领养	領養	lǐngyǎng	v.	to adopt (a child)	8
流产	流產	liúchǎn	n./v.	abortion, miscarriage; to abort, to miscarry	6
流动	流動	liúdòng	v./attr.	(of liquid or gas) to flow, to go from place to place; mobile	6
流入		liúrù	v.	to flow into, to drift into, to influx	8
率		lǜ	n./b.f.	rate, ratio	2

M

麦克风	麥克風	màikèfēng	n.	microphone	7
卖淫	賣淫	mài yín	v.o.	to prostitute oneself, to whore	8
蛮	蠻	mán	b.f./ adv.	quite, pretty, very	4
蔓延	蔓延	mànyán	v.	to extend, to creep, to spread	8
漫长	漫長	màncháng	adj.	very long, extensive, endless	2
门店	門店	méndiàn	n.	store	1
门槛儿	門檻兒	ménkǎnr	n.	threshold	7
门票	門票	ménpiào	n.	entrance ticket, admission ticket	2
萌动	萌動	méngdòng	v.	to germinate, to sprout	6
梦想	夢想	mèngxiǎng	n./v.	dream, illusion, fantasy; to dream	3
瞄准	瞄準	miáozhǔn	v(c)	to aim at	1
民警		mínjǐng	n.	people's police, policeman	7
明信片		míngxìnpiàn	n.	postcard	3
木工		mùgōng	n.	woodwork, carpentry	5

N

男女		nánnǚ	n.	men and women, male-female	8
难以置信	難以置信	nányǐzhìxìn	f.e.	unbelievable, incredible	4
脑	腦	nǎo	n./b.f.	brain, head, mind	7
内心	內心	nèixīn	n.	heart, bottom of the heart	5
年初		niánchū	n.	beginning of the year	7
酿	釀	niàng	v./b.f.	to make (wine); to lead to, to result in	8
宁静	寧靜	níngjìng	adj.	peaceful, tranquil, quiet	5
农户	農戶	nónghù	n.	peasant household	8
女孩		nǚhái	n.	girl	6

O

偶然		ǒurán	adj.	accidental, fortuitous, occasional	4

P

拍摄	拍攝	pāishè	v.	to shoot (a photograph, movie, etc.)	7
排斥		páichì	v.	to exclude, to repel	2
排队	排隊	pái duì	v.o.	to queue up, to line up	2
排解		páijiě	v.	to divert oneself from, to reconcile	5

判决	判決	pànjué	n./v.	court decision, judgment; to sentence	2
庞大	龐大	pángdà	adj.	big, huge, immense, enormous	7
培训	培訓	péixùn	v./n.	to cultivate, to train; training	7
配		pèi	v./b.f.	to allot; to provide with	1
配送		pèisòng	v.	to take a delivery	1
疲惫	疲憊	píbèi	adj.	weary, exhausted, tired out	5
譬如		pìrú	v.	for example, for instance, such as	7
嫖娼		piáo chāng	v.o.	to go whoring, to go to prostitutes	8
贫困	貧困	pínkùn	adj.	poor, impoverished	6
贫穷	貧窮	pínqióng	adj.	poor, needy, impoverished	8
平价	平價	píngjià	n.	parity, fair (state) price	1
平台	平臺	píngtái	n.	movable platform; terrace, flat roof	7
普查		pǔchá	v./n.	to census; general survey	8
普通话	普通話	pǔtōnghuà	n.	Mandarin Chinese	4

Q

妻		qī	n./b.f.	wife	8
期望		qīwàng	v./n.	to hope, to expect; expectation	3
棋		qí	n.	chess, board game	5
旗下		qíxià	n.	subordinate, those under one's command	1
契合		qìhé	v.	to agree with, to tally with	3
前提		qiántí	n.	premise, prerequisite	8
潜力	潛力	qiánlì	n.	latent capacity, potential, potentiality	7
强行	強行	qiángxíng	v.	to force, to do sth. using coercive methods	8
抢购	搶購	qiǎnggòu	v.	to rush to purchase	2
抢险	搶險	qiǎng xiǎn	v.o.	to rush to rescue, to rush to deal with an emergency	7
青春期		qīngchūnqī	n.	adolescence, puberty	6
穹顶	穹頂	qióngdǐng	n.	dome, vault	7
区别	區別	qūbié	v./n.	to distinguish, to differentiate; difference	3
娶		qǔ	v.	to marry (a woman)	8
趣闻	趣聞	qùwén	n.	interesting news, anecdotes	7
劝告	勸告	quàngào	v.	to advise; to urge; to recommend	6
缺失		quēshī	n.	lack of, deficiency, deletion, missing	6

R

| 人口与发展研究所 | 人口與發展研究所 | rénkǒu yǔ fāzhǎn yánjiūsuǒ | n.p. | institute for population and development | 8 |

人生		rénshēng	n.	life, human life	5
忍痛		rěn tòng	v.o.	(oft. unwillingly) to bear and suffer pain	8
刃		rèn	b.f./v.	blade; to kill with a sword or knife	7
妊娠		rènshēn	n.	pregnancy, maternity	6
日志	日誌	rìzhì	n.	journal, daily record, log	7

S

伤害	傷害	shānghài	v./n.	to harm, to hurt; injury	6
商界		shāngjiè	n.	business circles, commercial circles	5
奢侈		shēchǐ	adj.	luxury, extravagant	5
奢望		shēwàng	n./v.	extravagant hopes, wild wishes; to aim high	8
设立	設立	shèlì	v.	to establish, to set up, to found	7
射箭		shè jiàn	v.o.	to shoot arrows, to archery	5
身心		shēnxīn	n.	body and mind	5
生理		shēnglǐ	n.	physiology, physical	6
生殖		shēngzhí	n.	reproduction, procreation	6
声明	聲明	shēngmíng	v./n.	to announce; statement, declaration	2
失衡		shīhéng	v.	to lose balance	8
失调	失調	shī tiáo	v.o.	to lose balance	8
时机	時機	shíjī	n.	opportunity, occasion	5
时下	時下	shíxià	n.	currently, at present, right now	5
实习	實習	shíxí	v.	to practice, to do fieldwork	7
世世代代		shìshì-dàidài	f.e.	for generations, age after age	2
市府		shìfǔ	n.	municipal government	2
市区	市區	shìqū	n.	urban district, downtown	1
势必	勢必	shìbì	adv.	certainly will, be bound to	2
适龄	適齡	shìlíng	n.	of the right age	8
适宜	適宜	shìyí	adj.	suitable, appropriate, favorable	5
誓不罢休	誓不罷休	shìbúbàxiū	f.e.	to swear not to give up	8
收益		shōuyì	n.	income, profit, earnings, gains	1
受访者	受訪者	shòufǎngzhě	n.	interviewee	2
熟识	熟識	shúshi	v.	be well acquainted with, to know well	3
署名		shǔ míng	v.o.	to sign (a signature)	4
思潮		sīcháo	n.	trend of thought	2
诉诸	訴諸	sùzhū	v.	to resort to	3
孙女	孫女	sūnnǚ	n.	son's daughter, granddaughter	3
损耗	損耗	sǔnhào	v./n.	to cause loss; wear and tear	1

| 损伤 | 損傷 | sǔnshāng | n. | injury, harm, damage | 5 |

T

他乡	他鄉	tāxiāng	n.	a place far away from home, an alien land	8
踏入		tàrù	v(c)	to step into, to enter	6
太极	太極	tàijí	n.	Tai Ji (boxing)	5
太极拳	太極拳	tàijíquán	n.	traditional Chinese shadow boxing	5
瘫	癱	tān	v.	to be paralyzed	7
特地		tèdì	adv.	for a special purpose, specially	3
提到		tídào	v(c)	to mention, to refer to	2
替罪羊		tìzuìyáng	n.	scapegoat	2
调节	調節	tiáojié	v.	to regulate, to adjust	5
厅	廳	tīng	b.f./n.	hall	2
听众	聽眾	tīngzhòng	n.	audience, listeners	4
童		tóng	b.f./n.	child, under-age servant	6
投递	投遞	tóudì	v.	to deliver, to send	3
突发	突發	tūfā	v.	to burst out or occur suddenly	7

W

外出		wàichū	v.	to go out, to go out of town on business	8
完美		wánměi	adj.	perfect, flawless	4
顽疾	頑疾	wánjí	n.	chronic disease, recurring illness	8
网民	網民	wǎngmín	n.	internet user	4
危及		wēijí	v.	to endanger, to threat, to imperil	8
微博		wēibó	n.	microblog or tweets	4
为此	為此	wèicǐ	adv.	for this reason, therefore	2
违背	違背	wéibèi	v.	to violate, to go against	2
围棋	圍棋	wéiqí	n.	GO, encirclement chess	5
委员会	委員會	wěiyuánhuì	n.	committee, council	4
无形	無形	wúxíng	attr.	invisible, intangible	2
物极必反	物極必反	wùjí-bìfǎn	f.e.	Things will develop in the opposite direction when they become extreme	5
物流		wùliú	n.	logistics	1
物品		wùpǐn	n.	article, goods	1
误导	誤導	wùdǎo	v.	to mislead, to lead astray, to misguide	2
误区	誤區	wùqū	n.	pitfall, trap, misunderstanding	6
雾霾	霧霾	wùmái	n.	fog and haze, smog	7

X

简体	繁體	拼音	词类	英文	课
希腊文	希臘文	Xīlàwén	n.	Greek	4
媳妇	媳婦	xífù	n.	wife, son's wife, daughter-in-law	8
洗礼	洗禮	xǐlǐ	n.	baptism	2
细则	細則	xìzé	n.	detailed rules and regulations	7
先入为主	先入為主	xiān rù wéi zhǔ	f.e.	be prejudiced by first impressions; first impressions are firmly entrenched	7
现今	現今	xiànjīn	n.	nowadays	2
限度		xiàndù	n.	limitation, limit	1
限于	限於	xiànyú	v.	to be confined to, to be limited to	7
相约	相約	xiāngyuē	v.	to agree, to reach agreement	3
享有		xiǎngyǒu	v.	to enjoy (rights, privileges, etc.)	7
向往	向往	xiàngwǎng	v.	to yearn for, to look forward to	3
消除		xiāochú	v.	to eliminate, to dispel, to remove	2
小孩		xiǎohái	n.	child, kid	2
效率		xiàolǜ	n.	efficiency	3
效益		xiàoyì	n.	effectiveness, beneficial result, benefit	7
心灵	心靈	xīnlíng	n.	heart, soul	5
信件		xìnjiàn	n.	letter, mail	3
兴起	興起	xīngqǐ	v.	to rise, to spring up	2
性行为	性行為	xìngxíngwéi	n.	sexual behavior	6
性教育		xìngjiàoyù	n.	sex education	6
休闲	休閒	xiūxián	n.	leisure, relaxation	5
选票	選票	xuǎnpiào	n.	vote, ballot	2
削减	削減	xuējiǎn	v.	to cut down, to reduce	1
训	訓	xùn	v.	to train, to drill	5

Y

简体	繁體	拼音	词类	英文	课
压抑	壓抑	yāyì	v.	to constrain, to inhibit, to depress	3
炎症		yánzhèng	n.	inflammation, infection	6
演唱会	演唱會	yǎnchànghuì	n.	vocal concert	2
验	驗	yàn	v.	to inspect, to examine, to check	2
谣言	謠言	yáoyán	n.	rumor, canard	7
要么	要麼	yàome	conj.	or, either...or...	5
一旦		yídàn	conj.	in case (something happens), once	7
一己		yìjǐ	n.	self, oneself	7
一流		yīliú	attr.	first-rate, top-notch	1

生词索引

一阵子	一陣子	yízhènzi	n.	a period of time, a spell	5
依傍		yībàng	v.	to rely upon, to depend on	2
异性	異性	yìxìng	n.	heterosexual, opposite sex	6
意境		yìjìng	n.	artistic conception, artistic mood	5
毅力		yìlì	n.	willpower, tenacity, perseverance	4
盈		yíng	v./adj.	to be filled with, to be full of; to have a surplus of	8
尤为	尤為	yóuwéi	adv.	especially	6
邮寄	郵寄	yóujì	v.	to mail, to post	3
游离	游離	yóulí	v.	to drift away, to dissociate	2
有问必答	有問必答	yǒuwèn-bìdá	f.e.	to answer every question	4
有序		yǒuxù	v.	to be in order	7
有助		yǒuzhù	v.	to be helpful, to be conducive	5
余	餘	yú	num.	more than, surplus	8
瑜伽		yújiā	n.	yoga	5
园艺	園藝	yuányì	n.	horticulture, gardening, landscaping	5
员工	員工	yuángōng	n.	staff, personnel, clerk, worker	5
月底		yuèdǐ	n.	the end of a month	2
运营	運營	yùnyíng	v.	to be in operation, to operate (or run) in an organized way	1
运转	運轉	yùnzhuǎn	v.	to operate, to run, to revolve	5

Z

杂货	雜貨	záhuò	n.	sundry goods, groceries	1
再次		zàicì	adv.	second time, once more	2
增		zēng	v./b.f.	to increase, to add	1
扎实	扎實	zhāshi	adj.	solid, sound, strong	4
占据	佔據	zhànjù	v.	to occupy, to hold	2
掌声	掌聲	zhǎngshēng	n.	clapping, applause	4
遮遮掩掩		zhēzhē-yǎnyǎn	f.e.	to try to cover up	6
折射		zhéshè	v./n.	to reflect; reflection	8
正常		zhèngcháng	adj.	normal	6
证实	證實	zhèngshí	v.	to confirm, to verify	2
之外		zhīwài	n.	being excluded; besides, except, beyond	2
指定		zhǐdìng	v.	to appoint, to specify, to designate	3
致		zhì	v.	to result in	2
致使		zhìshǐ	v.	to cause, to lead to, to result in	8
智慧		zhìhuì	n.	wisdom, intelligence, wit	4

滞后	滯後	zhìhòu	v.	to lag behind, to delay; hysteresis	6
中产阶级	中產階級	zhōngchǎn jiējí	n.p.	middle class	2
主页	主頁	zhǔyè	n.	homepage	7
主因		zhǔyīn	n.	major cause, main reason	8
贮藏	貯藏	zhùcáng	v.	to store	3
祝愿	祝願	zhùyuàn	v.	to wish	3
转发	轉發	zhuǎnfā	v.	to repost, to relay, to retransmit	7
赚	賺	zhuàn	v.	to make a profit, to gain, to earn (money)	3
装修	裝修	zhuāngxiū	v./n.	to decorate; decoration	1
准则	準則	zhǔnzé	n.	norm, standard, criterion	2
滋长	滋長	zīzhǎng	v.	to grow, to develop	2
总裁	總裁	zǒngcái	n.	president (of a company)	1
走失		zǒushī	v.	to be lost, to be missing	7
座谈会	座談會	zuòtánhuì	n.	conference, symposium	4

专有名词索引

主课文部分

A

简体	繁体	拼音	英文	页
阿曼达·里普利	阿曼達·里普利	Āmàndá Lǐpǔlì	Amanda Ripley	4
阿姆斯特朗		Āmǔsītèlǎng	Lance Armstrong	5
艾米莉·迪金森		Àimǐlì Díjīnsēn	Emily Dickinson	4
爱白网	愛白網	Àibái Wǎng	a Chinese gay and lesbian website	2
奥林匹克	奧林匹克	Àolínpǐkè	Olympics	5
奥林匹克委员会	奧林匹克委員會	Àolínpǐkè Wěiyuánhuì	Olympic Committee	5
奥委会	奧委會	Àowěihuì	the abbreviation for Olympic Committee	5
奥运	奧運	Àoyùn	the Olympics	5

B

简体	繁体	拼音	英文	页
巴图辛·米昂甘巴雅	巴圖辛·米昂甘巴雅	Bātúxīn Mǐ'ánggānbāyǎ	a person's name	4
本·约翰逊	本·約翰遜	Běn Yuēhànxùn	Ben Johnson	5
苯丙胺		Běnbǐng'àn	amphetamine	5
比尔·盖茨	比爾·蓋茨	Bǐ'ěr Gàicí	Bill Gates	4
伯克利		Bókèlì	Berkley	4
布莱恩·威廉姆斯	布萊恩·威廉姆斯	Bùlái'ēn Wēiliánmǔsī	Brian Williams	7

C

简体	繁体	拼音	英文	页
春光乍泄		Chūnguāng Zhà Xiè	Happy Together	2
春秋		Chūnqiū	the Spring and Autumn Period (772-481B.C.)	2
刺青		Cìqīng	Tattoo	2

D

简体	繁体	拼音	英文	页
东宫西宫	東宮西宮	Dōnggōng Xīgōng	East Palace, West Palace	2

F

简体	繁体	拼音	英文	页
凤凰卫视	鳳凰衛視	Fènghuáng Wèishì	Phoenix Satellite Television Channel	2

G

谷歌		Gǔgē	Google	3
果壳网	果殼網	Guǒké Wǎng	a science and technology website in China	4

H

韩国	韓國	Hánguó	Republic of Korea	5
汉城	漢城	Hànchéng	Seoul, capital of the Republic of Korea	5
蝴蝶		Húdié	*Butterfly*	2

J

加利福尼亚	加利福尼亞	Jiālìfúníyà	California	2
加州		Jiāzhōu	California	2
剑桥大学	劍橋大學	Jiànqiáo Dàxué	University of Cambridge	3
旧金山	舊金山	Jiùjīnshān	San Francisco	2

K

卡特里娜		kǎtèlǐnà	Katrina	7
堪萨斯城	堪薩斯城	Kānsàsī Chéng	Kansas City	6
堪萨斯州	堪薩斯州	Kānsàsī Zhōu	Kansas	6
孔子		Kǒngzǐ	Confucius	4

L

蓝宇	藍宇	Lányǔ	*Lan Yu*	2
雷诺	雷諾	Léinuò	Reynolds	7
理查德·杜尔宾	理查德·杜爾賓	Lǐchádé Dù'ěrbīn	Richard Durbin	4
联合早报	聯合早報	Liánhé Zǎobào	*Lianhe Zaobao* (a Singapore newspaper)	8
刘磊	劉磊	Liú Lěi	a person's name	4
鲁豫	魯豫	Lǔyù	a person's name	2
路透社		Lùtòushè	Reuters News Agency	8
罗马	羅馬	Luómǎ	Rome	5
罗诉韦德案	羅訴韋德案	Luó Sù Wéidé Àn	Roe versus Wade Case	6

M

麻省理工学院	麻省理工學院	Máshěng Lǐgōng Xuéyuàn	Massachusetts Institute of Technology	4
马利昂·琼斯	馬利昂·瓊斯	Mǎlì'áng Qióngsī	Marion Jones	5
迈克·朗兹	邁克·朗茲	Màikè Lǎngzī	Mike Rounds	6

| 每日邮报 | 每日郵報 | Měirì Yóubào | *Daily Mail* | 3 |
| 蒙古国 | 蒙古國 | Ménggǔguó | Republic of Mongolia | 4 |

N

| 南达科他 | 南達科他 | Nándákētā | South Dokota | 6 |
| 南华早报 | 南華早報 | Nánhuá Zǎobào | *South China Morning Post* | 8 |

O

| 欧盟 | 歐盟 | Ōuméng | European Union | 1 |

P

| 皮尔·波特 | 皮爾·波特 | Pí'ěr Bōtè | Bill Porter | 8 |

Q

乔治·蒂勒	喬治·蒂勒	Qiáozhì Dìlè	George Taylor	6
乔治·皮特森	喬治·皮特森	Qiáozhì Pítèsēn	George Peterson	4
乔治亚理工大学	喬治亞理工大學	Qiáozhìyà Lǐgōng Dàxué	Georgia Institute of Technology	4
清华大学	清華大學	Qīnghuá Dàxué	Tsinghua University	4
全国广播公司	全國廣播公司	Quánguó Guǎngbō Gōngsī	National Broadcasting Company (NBC)	7

R

| 日本警视厅 | 日本警視廳 | Rìběn Jǐngshìtīng | Japan's National Police Agency | 3 |
| 瑞典 | | Ruìdiǎn | Sweden | 6 |

S

山东	山東	Shāndōng	Shandong (province)	4
圣路易斯	聖路易斯	Shènglùyìsī	Saint Louis, a city in Missouri, U.S.A	5
时代周刊	時代週刊	Shídài Zhōukān	*Time magazine*	4
士的宁	士的寧	Shìdìníng	strychnine	5
斯蒂芬·伯克		Sīdìfēn Bókè	Stephen Burks	7

T

| 托马斯·希克斯 | 托馬斯·希克斯 | Tuōmǎsī Xīkèsī | Thomas Hicks | 5 |

X

简体	繁體	Pinyin	English	#
希腊	希臘	Xīlà	Greece	4
悉尼		Xīní	Sydney, Australia	5
谢汉兰	謝漢蘭	Xiè Hànlán	a person's name	2
谢里·芬克拜	謝里·芬克拜	Xièlǐ Fēnkèbài	Sherri Finkbine	6
辛普森		Xīnpǔsēn	Simpsons	5
新奥尔良	新奧爾良	Xīn'ào'ěrliáng	New Orleans	7
徐葳		Xú Wēi	a person's name	4

Y

简体	繁體	Pinyin	English	#
亚马逊	亞馬遜	Yàmǎxùn	Amazon	3
延森		Yánsēn	Jensen	5
伊拉克		Yīlākè	Iraq	7
伊利诺伊	伊利諾伊	Yīlìnuòyī	Illinois	4
羽联	羽聯	Yǔlián	Badminton World Federation	5
越南		Yuènán	Vietnam	1

Z

简体	繁體	Pinyin	English	#
战国	戰國	Zhànguó	Warring States Period (476-221B.C.)	2
中央电视台	中央電視臺	Zhōngyāng Diànshìtái	China Central Television (CCTV)	2

副课文部分

A

简体	繁體	Pinyin	English	#
阿里		Ālǐ	the abbreviation for Alibaba company	5
阿里巴巴		Ālǐbābā	Alibaba company	5
安徽		Ānhuī	Anhui (province)	7
安庆师范学院	安慶師範學院	Ānqìng Shīfàn Xuéyuàn	Anqing Teachers College	7
奥巴马	奧巴馬	Àobāmǎ	Obama	2

专有名词索引

B

| 北京东四妇产医院 | 北京東四婦產醫院 | Běijīng Dōngsì Fùchǎn Yīyuàn | Beijing Dongsi Obstetrical and Gynecological Hospital | 6 |

C

柴静	柴静	Chái Jìng	*a person's name*	7
陈吉宁	陳吉寧	Chén Jíníng	*a person's name*	4
程江涛	程江濤	Chéng Jiāngtāo	*a person's name*	7
崔颖	崔穎	Cuī Yǐng	*a person's name*	6

G

| 盖洛普 | 蓋洛普 | Gàiluòpǔ | Gallup, Inc. | 2 |

H

| 何安瑞 | | Hé Ānruì | Arie Hoekman | 6 |
| 胡玉娣 | | Hú Yùdì | *a person's name* | 7 |

J

剑桥	劍橋	Jiànqiáo	Cambridge	2
今日头条	今日頭條	Jīnrì Tóutiáo	*Today's Headline News*	7
金融时报	金融時報	Jīnróng Shíbào	*Financial Times*	1

L

雷布·雷西		Léibù Léixī	Ray Bracy	1
联合国	聯合國	liánhéguó	the United Nations (U.N.)	6
脸书	臉書	Liǎnshū	Facebook	4
陆克文	陸克文	Lù Kèwén	Kevin Rudd	4

M

马克·扎克伯格	馬克·扎克伯格	Mǎkè Zhākèbógé	Mark Zuckerberg	4
马萨诸塞	馬薩諸塞	Mǎsàzhūsài	Massachusetts	2
马云	馬雲	Mǎ Yún	*a person's name*, founder of Alibaba	5
美国广播公司	美國廣播公司	Měiguó Guǎngbō Gōngsī	American Broadcasting Company (ABC)	2
民主党	民主黨	Mínzhǔdǎng	Democratic Party	2

N

简体	繁體	Pinyin	English	Lesson
南京		Nánjīng	Nanjing (capital of Jiangsu Province)	3
南开大学	南開大學	Nánkāi Dàxué	Nankai University	8

Q

简体	繁體	Pinyin	English	Lesson
清华	清華	Qīnghuá	Tsinghua University, China	4

R

简体	繁體	Pinyin	English	Lesson
人人网	人人網	Rénrén Wǎng	RENN, Chinese Facebook	7

S

简体	繁體	Pinyin	English	Lesson
山姆会员店	山姆會員店	Shānmǔ Huìyuán Diàn	Sam's Club	1
上帝		Shàngdì	God	2
上海交通大学	上海交通大學	Shànghǎi Jiāotōng Dàxué	Shanghai Jiao Tong University	5
社会蓝皮书	社會藍皮書	Shèhuì Lánpíshū	Social Blue Book	8
沈阳	瀋陽	Shěn Yáng	a person's name	7
圣经	聖經	Shèngjīng	the Bible	2

T

简体	繁體	Pinyin	English	Lesson
腾讯	騰訊	Téngxùn	Tencent, a Chinese company	7
推特		Tuītè	Twitter	7

W

简体	繁體	Pinyin	English	Lesson
微软	微軟	Wēiruǎn	Microsoft	4
微信		Wēixìn	WeChat	7
文兴乡	文興鄉	Wénxīng Xiāng	Wenxing County	8
沃尔玛	沃爾瑪	Wò'ěrmǎ	Walmart	1

X

简体	繁體	Pinyin	English	Lesson
忻州		Xīnzhōu	Xinzhou City in Shanxi Province	7
新浪		Xīnlàng	Sina, a Chinese website	7
宣威市		Xuānwēi Shì	Xuanwei City in Yunnan Province	8

Y

原新		Yuán Xīn	*a person's name*	8
云南	雲南	Yúnnán	Yunnan Province	8

Z

张一鸣	張一鳴	Zhāng Yīmíng	*a person's name*	7
赵家村	趙家村	Zhàojiā Cūn	Zhao Village	8
赵文杰	趙文傑	Zhào Wénjié	*a person's name*	5
中国社会科学院	中國社會科學院	Zhōngguó Shèhuì Kēxuéyuàn	Chinese Academy of Social Sciences (CASS)	8

Today's World II
Select Readings of Chinese Spotlight News

Workbook
·练习本·

今日世界面面观
汉语焦点新闻选读
下册

王 颖　王志军　徐丽莎　◎编著

北京大学出版社

CONTENTS
目 录

第 1 课

经济改革如何与危机赛跑 /1

第 2 课

浅析中国同性恋现象 /6

第 3 课

3D打印与未来生活 /11

第 4 课

在线大学：在网络时代实现"有教无类"的梦想 /16

第 5 课

奥运会与兴奋剂 /23

第 6 课

道德还是自由：美国堕胎合法化之争 /28

第 7 课

美国金牌主播因"说谎门"而"下课" /35

第 8 课

外媒热议：中国开放"二胎"政策 /41

第 1 课　经济改革如何与危机赛跑

一、请用英文解释下列词的意思
Please give the meanings of the following words in English

外企　　　　　　方式　　　　　　欧式

势力　　　　　　形势

暴力　　　　　　下跌　　　　　　沸点

时机　　　　　　创造性

竞争力　　　　　　老年化

二、词汇搭配
Match the following two groups of words or phrases

爆发	消费
探求	这个难得的机遇
把握	今后的发展
纵观	金融危机
刺激	城镇医疗事业
致力于	新的合作方式

三、区分下面词汇的用法并完成填空

◆ Please note the different usages of the following words and fill in the blanks

1. 把握、握

（把握 is usually used in a more abstract sense and is a written/formal expression while 握 is often used in a more concrete sense and is a spoken/informal expression.）

① _____机遇；_____手

② _____节奏；_____笔；_____方向

2. 取胜、胜

（取胜 is usually used in a more abstract sense and is a written/formal expression while 胜 is often used in a more concrete sense and is a spoken/informal expression. 取胜 cannot take an object, but 胜 can.）

① 这次篮球比赛我们的校队_____了。

② 只有充分了解敌方，才能在战争中_____。

③ 在这次数学竞赛中，北京八中_____了北京四中。

④ 要想在未来的经济竞争中_____，人才的培养和科技的发展十分重要。

四、选词填空

◆ Choose the most appropriate word and fill in the blanks

所	并	由	于
既	为	而且	以来

1. 据分析，老人死_____突发性心脏病。

2. 北京不仅是中国的政治中心，_____是文化中心。

3. 由于家长的溺爱，独生子女_____缺乏独立生活的能力，也缺乏社会交际能力。

4. 她是_____公司挑选出来承担这项工作的。

5. 据报道,英国一家超市_____售的巧克力含有对人体有害的病菌。

6. 她照顾那个小女孩_____报了警,最后找到了小女孩的父母。

7. 自从上大学_____,他一直坚持每天跑步。

8. 学生还是要以学习_____主要任务,打工是次要的。

五、句段分析

◆ *Sentence analysis*

1. 找出下列句子的主语、谓语和宾语(Please indicate the subject, predicate, and object in the following sentences)

   (1) 在经济危机的威胁下,如何保持经济的稳定和可持续发展,是当今中国所面临的一个重大挑战。

   主语:　　　　　谓语:　　　　　宾语:

   (2) 出口遇到的问题一方面是由人民币升值造成的成本优势下降。

   主语:　　　　　谓语:　　　　　宾语:

2. 把下列句子翻译成英文(Translate the following sentences into English)

   (1) 政府应该保障一个公开、透明的市场,为经济发展提供一个良好的环境。

(2) 日本政府高达56.8万亿日元的经济刺激计划中，有6万亿日元用于绿色能源产业的发展。

六、小作文

◆ Short essay

在你看来，2008年金融危机后，美国和欧洲国家的经济面临着什么样的挑战？近几年来欧美的经济是否有所改善？中国经济对这些国家、地区，以及世界经济的影响是什么？

（200-300字，请在你的作文中尽量用上本课所学的生词和句型结构。200-300 characters; please do your best to use the words and grammar patterns learned in this lesson.）

Lesson 1

第1课 经济改革如何与危机赛跑

第 2 课　浅析中国同性恋现象

一、请用英文解释下列词的意思
◆ *Please give the meanings of the following words in English*

异地恋　　　　　　　　　　自信心

安全感

自我意识　　　　　　　　　跨文化

跨学科　　　　　　　　　　非营利组织

非官方

二、选词填空
◆ *Choose the most appropriate word and fill in the blanks*

| 属于……范畴　　发出……感慨　　举行……仪式 |

1. 我国民族传统体育_____民俗文化的_____，其中蕴含着深厚的文化内涵。

2. 那些参加奥运会的运动员们_____了同样的_____："获得奥运会冠军太难了！"

3. 面对巨大的贫富差距，很多人_____这个社会不公的_____。

4. 美国总统在白宫_____了隆重的_____欢迎中国贵宾。

5. 这些问题_____心理学_____，你去看看相关的书籍。

6. 听说你们要结婚了，在哪儿_____结婚_____？

三、选词填空

♦ *Choose the most appropriate word and fill in the blanks*

1. 他说的_____是对的，我们就要听。

   a. 虽然　　　　b. 既然　　　　c. 竟然　　　　d. 即使

2. _____怕受到歧视，很多同性恋者不敢暴露身份。

   a. 只有　　　　b. 虽然　　　　c. 由于　　　　d. 即使

3. _____估计，这家公司今年损失高达 3000 万美元。

   a. 以　　　　　b. 为　　　　　c. 对　　　　　d. 据

4. 这次事故只_____总经理有关，其他人不承担责任。

   a. 同　　　　　b. 为　　　　　c. 据　　　　　d. 被

5. 希望你以身体_____重，不要过分悲伤。

   a. 同　　　　　b. 为　　　　　c. 于　　　　　d. 及

6. 不要_____他的甜言蜜语所欺骗，要多观察他的所做所为。

   a. 于　　　　　b. 与　　　　　c. 被　　　　　d. 同

7. 月薪一万元_____刚毕业不久的大学生来说，确实是不小的数目。

   a. 与　　　　　b. 同　　　　　c. 为　　　　　d. 对于

四、理解下列句子，选择正确答案

♦ *Carefully read each of the following sentences and among the four given choices, select one that has the same meaning with the sentence*

1. 绝大多数的同性恋者不得不隐匿自己的身份，仍然戴着面具生活。

   a. 很多同性恋者要把身份隐藏起来。

b. 大多数同性恋者不用隐藏自己的身份。

c. 大多数同性恋者用面具隐藏自己。

d. 在日常生活中，大多数同性恋者戴着面具。

2. 在中国，尽管同性恋依然是一个非主流的禁忌话题，但是中国社会对同性恋的宽容度正在逐步扩大。

a. 虽然人们都在公开谈论同性恋的问题，但是大多数不支持同性恋。

b. 虽然中国不公开谈论同性恋的问题，但是越来越多的人对同性恋表示理解。

c. 虽然人们不公开谈论同性恋的问题，但是多数人支持同性恋结婚。

d. 虽然中国社会对同性恋越来越不宽容，但是人们依然公开谈论有关同性恋的话题。

五、句段分析

◆ *Sentence analysis*

1. 找出下列句子的主语、谓语和宾语（Please indicate the subject, predicate, and object in the following sentences）

   (1) 加州知名华裔女作家谢汉兰与伴侣在旧金山市政厅司法官的主持下举行了结婚仪式。

   主语：　　　　　　谓语：　　　　　　宾语：

   (2) 2005年，作为中国政府主流媒体代表的中央电视台播出了与同性恋有关的节目《以生命的名义》。

   主语：　　　　　　谓语：　　　　　　宾语：

2. 把下列句子翻译成英文（Translate the following sentences into English）

(1) 中国文化源远流长，中国人对自己的主流文化很有信心，从不担心被非主流文化所影响。

(2) 由于在宣传上常把艾滋病与同性恋相联系，加深了一些缺乏相关知识的人们对同性恋的歧视。

六、小作文

◆ *Short essay*

在中国，同性恋者面对哪些方面的压力？中国公众对同性恋的接纳程度比较高，历史和文化的原因有哪些？在美国，同性恋者有什么压力？你对同性恋的看法是什么？

（200-300 字，请在你的作文中尽量用上本课所学的生词和句型结构。200-300 characters; please do your best to use the words and grammar patterns learned in this lesson.）

第3课　3D打印与未来生活

一、请用英文解释下列词的意思
◆ Please give the meanings of the following words in English

装饰品 _____　　茶具 _____　　海域 _____

复发 _____　　洗碗机 _____

饭卡 _____　　文学家 _____

二、词汇搭配
◆ Match the following two groups of words or phrases

破获	教育
普及	假肢
推出	后果
采纳	凶杀案
致命的	步伐
柔软的	意见
蹒跚的	新产品

三、区分下面词汇的用法并完成填空

◆ *Please note the different usages of the following words and fill in the blanks*

1. 存储、存

(存储 is usually used in a more abstract sense, is a written/formal expression, and means "to store"or "storage, memorizing"; 存 is often used in a more concrete sense, is a spoken/informal expression, and means "to store, keep, deposit". In addition, while 存储 can be used as both verb and noun, 存 can only be used as a verb.)

① _____包；光盘_____；_____安全；

② 网络_____；_____钱；_____衣服；_____管理

2. 开启、开

(开启 is usually used in a more abstract sense and is a written/formal expression while 开 is often used in a more concrete sense and is a spoken/informal expression.)

① _____车；_____新时代

② _____知识的宝库；_____窗；_____门

四、找出与阴影词语最接近的解释

◆ *Choose the expression that is closest in meaning to the shaded word or phrase*

_____ 1. 3D打印能打印婚纱、戒指、房子和车子，它真的"无所不能"吗？

    a. 没有什么不能做到的   b. 什么都不行   c. 什么都知道

_____ 2. 很多人的梦想是能到世界各地旅行，这并不是"遥不可及"的。

    a. 路太远了   b. 不能实现   c. 很容易实现

_____ 3. 电影《Hachi: A Dog's Tale》的故事让我 感动不已 。

　　a. 一直很感动　　b. 不再感动　　　　c. 无法感动

_____ 4. 机器人服务员首次 亮相 中国的麦当劳餐厅。

　　a. 在公共场所出现　　b. 很明亮　　c. 不清楚

_____ 5.他的病是 先天 的，很难治好。

　　a. 出生以后才有的　　b. 很早以前得的　　c. 生来就有的

_____ 6.在纽约和上海，你都可以租公共自行车出行，非常 便捷 。

　　a. 方便　　　b. 快速　　　c. 便宜

五、选词填空

◆ *Choose the most appropriate word and fill in the blanks*

| 该 | 当中 | 到 | 之 |

1. 对全球近1.4万IT安全专业人士的调查显示，在过去的几年里，女性在IT安全工作人员_____的比例只有10%。

2. Apple watch开启了一个新时代，_____产品能够用语音控制电视。

3. 我认为世界上最难的职业_____一是总统的工作。

4. 2011年日本大海啸造成的损失大_____无法估计。

六、句段分析

◆ *Sentence analysis*

1. 找出下列句子的主语、谓语和宾语（Please indicate the subject, predicate, and object in the following sentences）

　　(1) 3D打印技术的发展为人们的生活开启了一扇通往无限可能的大门。

　　主语：　　　　　谓语：　　　　　宾语：

(2) 英国剑桥大学研究人员用3D技术来修复老鼠的视网膜细胞。

主语：　　　　　　谓语：　　　　　　宾语：

2. 把下列句子翻译成英文（Translate the following sentences into English）

(1) 在他们的这场婚礼中所用到的灯具、喜糖盒、筷子、首饰，甚至包括结婚戒指、手捧花、婚纱等等全部都是由他们自己设计并由3D打印制成的。

(2) 3D打印也就是人们常说的增材制造，即利用数字文件通过3D打印机制造3D实物的先进制造和设计流程。

七、小作文

◆ Short essay

如果你有一台3D打印机，你想打印什么？它对人们的未来生活会造成什么影响？

（200-300字，请在你的作文中尽量用上本课所学的生词和句型结构。200-300 characters; please do your best to use the words and grammar patterns learned in this lesson.）

在线大学：在网络时代实现"有教无类"的梦想

一、请用英文解释下列词的意思

♦ Please give the meanings of the following words in English

微型 _____ 免税 _____

记者 _____ 五星级 _____ 首演 _____

重建 _____ 证书 _____ 互动 _____

二、词汇搭配

♦ Match the following two groups of words or phrases

维护	准则
禁止	法案
违背	威胁
提出	权利
签署	堕胎
受到	挑战
缺乏	时代
超越	动力

三、区分下面词汇的用法并完成填空

◆ *Please note the different usages of the following words and fill in the blanks*

1. 遥远、远

(遥远 and 远 both mean "distant, far away", but 遥远 is usually used more in written/formal expression, while 远 is often used in both written and spoken/informal expression. In addition, 遥远 usually modifies disyllabic words, and 远 usually modifies monosyllabic words. 远 can be negated by 不，while 遥远 cannot be negated by 不 directly without 并. 不遥远 is not correct, while 并不遥远 is correct. Lastly, 远 can be a complement, while 遥远 cannot.)

① 我们无法预测_____的未来，所以要把握好现在。

② 北京离天津有多_____？

③ 老师望着_____处，好像在思考着什么。

④ 妻子把丈夫送到门外，一直看到他走得很_____才回来。

⑤ 这些孩子来自_____的非洲，需要特别的关心和照顾。

2. 方式、方法

（方式 and 方法 both mean "way". 方式 emphasizes the way to go about things, usually a formed pattern, convention, or a particular way of doing things and is often combined with 生活 or 工作. 方法 emphasizes the method or solution to certain problems and is frequently combined with 思想, 学习, 训练, etc.）

① 我舅舅长期生活在偏僻的农村，不习惯城市的生活_____。

② 他纠正别人的错误很有_____，总是让对方能够接受。

③ 有人说，中国人的思维_____跟西方人很不一样。

④ 请告诉我你记汉字有什么好_____。

3. 替代、替

(替代 and 替 both are verbs that mean "to replace, to substitute", but 替代 is usually used more in written/formal expression, while 替 is often used in spoken/informal expression. In addition, 替 can be a preposition that means "for", while 替代 does not function as a preposition.)

① 你去邮局的时候，顺便_____我买几张邮票好吗？

② 知道你已经被那家大公司录用了，我们都_____你高兴。

③ 在孩子眼中，妈妈的角色是不可_____的。

④ 这家飞机公司正在研制新式发动机以_____老式发动机。

4. 缺乏、缺少

(缺乏 and 缺少 are both verbs that mean "to be short of, to lack"; 缺乏 can only take abstract objects, and the objects cannot be modified by numbers, while 缺少 can take both abstract and concrete objects, and its objects can be modified by numbers.)

① 一位优秀的领导人绝对不能_____号召力和判断力。

② 加州今年特别_____雨水，全年干旱，可能农业要减产。

③ 这个句子的结尾_____一个句号，请加上。

④ 你不能改正错误是因为你_____对这个问题的正确认识。

四、找出与阴影词语最接近的解释

◆ *Choose the expression that is closest in meaning to the shaded word or phrase*

_____ 1. 有了智能手机以后，我就可以 随时随地 上网了。

a. 随着时间和地点   b. 在任何时间、任何地点   c. 选择时间、地点

_____ 2. 大多数同学对这个话题不感兴趣，只有他 兴趣盎然 地说个不停。

　　a. 兴趣浓厚　　　b. 不感兴趣　　　c. 兴趣不太大

_____ 3. 他在女孩子面前总是 侃侃而谈，在男孩子面前则默默无言。

　　a. 信心十足地说个不停　　b. 大声说话　　c. 说话不多

_____ 4. 教育的最高理想就是 有教无类，我们应该向着这个方向努力。

　　a. 有的人没有受教育机会　　b. 任何人都可以受到教育

　　c. 不同背景的人受到不同的教育

_____ 5. 他去国外留学四年，回来后大不一样，令人 刮目相看。

　　a. 难以改变对他的看法　　b. 增加了对他的好奇心　　c. 重新看待他

五、选词填空

◆ Choose the most appropriate word and fill in the blanks

| 不论 | 于是 | 于 | 为 |
| 在于 | 之所以 | | |

1. _____我做什么，在她眼里都是对的。

2. 我_____这么做是因为那时候我不知道事情的真相。

3. 你学不好汉字的原因_____你从不练习书写。

5. 我学习中文是受了姐姐的影响，姐姐要来中国留学，_____我也就来了。

6. 我开始弹钢琴的时候完全是出_____好奇心，后来就越弹越喜欢了。

7. 2008年奥巴马被选_____美国总统，入住白宫。

六、句段分析

◆ Sentence analysis

1. 找出下列句子的主语、谓语和宾语（Please indicate the subject, predicate, and object in the following sentences）

   (1) 近年来，在线大学"慕课"（MOOC）的兴办又一次张起了"教育平等""精英教育平民化"的大旗。

   主语：　　　　　谓语：　　　　　宾语：

   (2) 2012年11月比尔·盖茨基金会向世界上最大的在线学习首创机构edX投资一百万美元。

   主语：　　　　　谓语：　　　　　宾语：

   (3) 刚从美国回到清华大学的年轻学者徐葳，从伯克利大学带回了一门名为"云计算与软件工程"的在线课程。

   主语：　　　　　谓语：　　　　　宾语：

2. 把下列句子翻译成英文（Translate the following sentences into English）

   (1) 这场席卷全球的"慕课教学实践"使世界上最优质的教育传播到地球最偏远的角落，也让"随时随地"的终身学习不再遥远。

(2) "慕课"教学不仅向全球免费提供知名高校的优质课程，而且正在通过课堂与在线混合模式重构校园教育。

(3) "慕课"预示着教育领域有发生颠覆性变革的可能性，向那些每年收五万美元学费的大学提出一个挑战：如果知识可以从互联网免费获得，你得提供什么样的教育才值这个钱？

七、小作文

◆ Short essay

"慕课"教学有什么优点和缺点？你注册过免费网络课程吗？你对网络课程有什么看法？

（200-300字，请在你的作文中尽量用上本课所学的生词和句型结构。200-300 characters; please do your best to use the words and grammar patterns learned in this lesson.）

第 5 课 奥运会与兴奋剂

一、请用英文解释下列词的意思

◆ Please give the meanings of the following words in English

银器　　　　　杀虫剂　　　　　广告牌

食物　　　　　水手　　　　　　政坛

二、词汇搭配

◆ Match the following two groups of words or phrases

三、区分下面词汇的用法并完成填空

◆ Please note the different usages of the following words and fill in the blanks

1. 剥夺、夺

（剥夺 is usually used in a more abstract sense and is a written/formal expression while 夺 is often used in a more concrete sense and is a spoken/informal expression.）

① _____资格；_____枪

② _____头衔；_____刀；_____权利

2. 建立、建

（建立 is usually used in a more abstract sense and is a written/formal expression while 建 is often used in a more concrete sense and is a spoken/informal expression.）

① _____信心；_____工厂

② _____制度；_____家庭；_____小学

四、找出与阴影词语最接近的解释

◆ Choose the expression that is closest in meaning to the shaded word or phrase

_____ 1. 中华酒文化 源远流长 。

a. 路很远　　　b. 有着很长的历史和传统　　　c. 河流很长

_____ 2. 期末考试后，学生都 精疲力尽 。

a. 非常累　　　b. 没有能力　　　c. 心情不好

_____ 3. 做任何事只要 坚持不懈 ，就会成功。

a. 一直努力　　　b. 不轻松　　　c. 不努力

_____ 4. 练习太极拳的好处 不胜枚举 。

a. 不多　　　b. 太少　　　c. 很多

_____ 5. 总统的 丑闻 被新闻披露了出来。

a. 新闻　　　b. 不好的消息　　　c. 长得丑的消息

_____ 6. 学习的道路没有 尽头 。

a. 起点　　　　b. 终点　　　　c. 中间点

五、选词填空

◆ *Choose the most appropriate word and fill in the blanks*

| 为 | 随之 | 以 | 因……而…… | 只要……就…… |

1. 四川火锅_____麻辣_____闻名。

2. 他因为一件小事就自杀了，这让人们大_____震惊。

3. 你_____不再吃炸鸡_____能减肥。

4. 城市私家车数量不断增加，交通越来越拥挤，交通事故也_____增加。

5. 这个图书馆每年二分之一的资金_____购买新出的书籍。

六、句段分析

◆ *Sentence analysis*

1. 找出下列句子的主语、谓语和宾语(Please indicate the subject, predicate, and object in the following sentences)

(1) 反兴奋剂和兴奋剂之间的斗争也像是猫捉老鼠。

主语：　　　　　谓语：　　　　　宾语：

(2) 专家们将进行各种化验来检测选手们是否服用了此前查不出来的违禁药物。

主语：　　　　　谓语：　　　　　宾语：

2. 把下列句子翻译成英文(Translate the following sentences into English)

(1) 现代奥运史上最早的服用兴奋剂的事件发生在1904年的美国圣路易斯第三届现代奥林匹克运动会上。

(2) 在澳大利亚，几乎有三分之一的运动员表示会考虑使用兴奋剂提高成绩。

七、小作文

◆ **Short essay**

人们往往在利益的驱使下，做不该做的事儿。你认为奥运会服用兴奋剂的现象会彻底消除吗？为了减少或消除服用兴奋剂的事件，奥林匹克委员会应该采取什么措施？每个国家应该做些什么？

（200–300字，请在你的作文中尽量用上本课所学的生词和句型结构。200–300 characters; please do your best to use the words and grammar patterns learned in this lesson.）

Lesson 5
奥运会与兴奋剂

第 6 课　道德还是自由：美国堕胎合法化之争

一、请用英文解释下列词的意思

♦ Please give the meanings of the following words in English

发言人 _____　　婚期 _____　　反政府 _____

草药 _____　　畸形 _____

强化 _____

二、词汇搭配

♦ Match the following two groups of words or phrases

剥夺	准则
禁止	法案
违背	威胁
实施	权利
签署	堕胎
受到	手术
解决	争端
公布	公投
发表	声明
发动	消息

28

三、区分下面词汇的用法并完成填空

◆ *Please note the different usages of the following words and fill in the blanks*

1. 采取、采用

（采取 and 采用 are verbs that mean "to adopt, to use", but 采取 usually takes abstract objects, while 采用 can take both concrete and abstract objects.）

① 我们两个球队虽然是竞争对手，但是相互之间不应该_____敌对的态度。

② 工厂决定_____新技术，提高生产效率。

③ 政府必须_____强有力的措施，控制有害气体的排放。

④ 他的计划一旦被_____，会给我们公司造成不利的局面。

2. 受到、遭受

（受到 and 遭受 both are verbs that mean "to meet with, to receive", but 遭受 can only take objects that are negative or have bad connotations, such as disaster or misfortune, while 受到 can take positive, neutral, or negative objects. The objects for both verbs cannot be monosyllabic, and are usually disyllabic.）

① 那个学生上课表现好，学习努力，_____了老师的表扬。

② 听了他的演讲，使我_____了很大的启发。

③ 一个人一生总是会_____一些挫折和失败。

④ 这个地区今年八月_____了洪水的侵袭。

3. 将、把

（将 and 把 both are prepositions used to position the object of a verb before the verb. They each indicate the disposal of the object or how the action of the verb affects the object. 将 is used in written/formal expression, while 把 is often used in more spoken/

informal expression. In addition, 将 can also mean 拿 or 用 and is often used in idiomatic expressions.）

① 很多人都在讨论是否_____堕胎合法化。

② 那位老师_____我的笔记本拿走了。

③ 你们不要_____问题复杂化。

④ 为了赌博，他不但_____所有的积蓄花光，还跟朋友借了一大笔钱。

⑤ ____心比心，我非常理解你的感受。

⑥ 这次我一定把任务完成，____功折罪。

4. 显示、显得

（显示 and 显得 are both verbs. 显示 means "to show, to display, to demonstrate" while 显得 means "to look, to seem, to appear". 显示 can only take nouns as its objects, while 显得 can only take adjectives.）

① 近两年来中国经济_____了很强的增长势头。

② 如果把这些书到处乱放，房间会_____非常拥挤。

③ 你穿上这条裙子，带上帽子，_____更加漂亮了。

④ 这次画展_____了这一代画家高超的艺术水平。

5. 更加、更

（更加 and 更 are both adverbs that mean "more, even more"; 更加 is usually used more in written/formal expression, while 更 is often used in spoken/informal expression. In addition, 更加 usually does not modify monosyllabic adjectives and verbs, while 更 can.）

① 这里的风景比那里_____美。

② 今年的收入很好，希望明年_____上一层楼。

Lesson 6

第6课 道德还是自由：美国堕胎合法化之争

③ 来到中国以后，他 _____ 感到学习中文的重要性。

④ 这件事以后，我的老师比以前 _____ 严格。

四、找出与阴影词语最接近的解释

◆ Choose the expression that is closest in meaning to the shaded word or phrase

_____ 1. 在美国关于枪支管制的争论 愈演愈烈 。

　a. 越来越少　　　b. 越来越激烈　　　c. 越来越严肃

_____ 2. 学校采用的教学法与全国各地的教学法 背道而驰 。

　a. 做法相同　　　b. 做法完全不同　　　c. 做法基本相近

_____ 3. 这些学生 不顾禁令 ，仍然在大街上喝酒，结果遭到逮捕。

　a. 不服从法令　　　b. 不愿意受到管教　　　c. 不会受到处罚

五、选词填空

◆ Choose the most appropriate word and fill in the blanks

而	否则	无异于	被视为	该
对……而言	于	为	对	

1. 每天喝酒吸烟 _____ 慢性自杀，应该马上戒掉。

2. 这个学生因为论文质量高 _____ 得了奖。

3. 他每天锻炼三个小时，_____ 身体不会这样健康。

4. 任何一个有残疾的人都不能 _____ 无能。

5. _____ 父母来说，孩子的健康和教育应该是最重要的。

6. 老师们对王明的评语是：_____ 生品学兼优，成绩优异。

7. _____ 教学 _____ ，这个课堂活动并没有实现教学目标。

8. 参加各种课外活动有利_____培养学生的兴趣爱好。

9. _____加快经济的发展，政府采取了免税政策。

六、句段分析

◆ Sentence analysis

1. 找出下列句子的主语、谓语和宾语(Please indicate the subject, predicate, and object in the following sentences)

   (1) 在世界历史上，对于文明的真正考验是看人们怎样对待社会上最弱势和无助的群体。

   主语：　　　　　谓语：　　　　　宾语：

   (2) 2009年5月31日，因提供晚期堕胎而颇具争议性的美国医生乔治·蒂勒在堪萨斯州堪萨斯城遭人枪杀。

   主语：　　　　　谓语：　　　　　宾语：

2. 把下列句子翻译成英文(Translate the following sentences into English)

   (1) 经营南达科他州唯一堕胎诊所的"家庭计划联盟"称，这项法律"悍然违宪"，极其危险，而且得不到大多数美国人的支持。

（2）无论美国人在像堕胎这样的富有争议的问题上分歧有多大，都不应该用暴力这样恶劣的行动来解决争端。

七、小作文

◆ *Short essay*

你觉得堕胎应该禁止还是合法化？为什么？

（200–300 字，请在你的作文中尽量用上本课所学的生词和句型结构。200–300 characters; please do your best to use the words and grammar patterns learned in this lesson.）

第7课 美国金牌主播因"说谎门"而"下课"

一、请用英文解释下列词的意思

Please give the meanings of the following words in English

受害　　　　　　　　　　　　　停薪

洗衣机　　　　　　　　　　　　失信

导弹　　　　　　　　　　　　　艳照门

新闻界　　　　　　　　　　　　可信度

曝光率

二、词汇搭配

Match the following two groups of words or phrases

虚假　　　　人士
重磅　　　　伎俩
严厉　　　　主播
惯用　　　　谎话
辉煌　　　　炸弹
知名　　　　处罚
低级　　　　事业
显赫　　　　报道

三、区分下面词汇的用法并完成填空

◆ *Please note the different usages of the following words and fill in the blanks*

1. 经历、经验

（Both 经历 and 经验 are nouns that mean "experience"; however, 经验 emphasizes the knowledge or skills gained from past experience, while 经历 refers to personal experience that a person has gone through. In addition, 经历 can function as a verb, but 经验 cannot.）

① 你中文学得这么好，能不能说说你的_____。

② 这位老师很有_____，我们都得向他请教。

③ 这本书写的是他过去在中国工作的_____。

④ 50后的那代人都_____了"文化大革命"。

2. 回顾、回忆

（Both 回顾 and 回忆 are verbs that mean "to recall, to look back"; however, 回顾 is usually a written/formal expression, while 回忆 can be used as both a written and spoken/informal expression. In addition, 回顾 refers to recalling personal experience or national/important social events in the past, but 回忆 refers only to recalling personal events. Moreover, 回忆 can be a noun, but 回顾 cannot.）

① 你说的这个事，我实在一点儿也_____不起来了。

② _____中国改革开放的二十年历程，使我们对未来的经济前景充满信心。

③ 在中国留学的两年，给我留下了美好的_____。

④ 要探讨中美关系，我们首先要_____一下中美关系的建立过程。

3. 给予、给

(Both 给予 and 给 are verbs that mean "to give". 给予 is usually used in a more abstract sense, is a written/formal expression, and takes verbs as its objects. 给 is usually used for concrete objects, is a spoken/informal expression, and usually take nouns as its objects.)

① 对于那些生活比较困难的学生，老师_____了很大的帮助和支持。

② 我们把报告交上去很长时间了，可是他们到现在还没有_____明确的答复。

③ 他爸爸_____了他一台笔记本电脑。

④ 这次作文老师_____了她一个很高的分数。

四、找出与阴影词语最接近的解释

◆ Choose the expression that is closest in meaning to the shaded word or phrase

_____ 1. 我刚才从 九死一生 的危险中奇迹般地逃了出来，现在还惊恐万分。

　　a. 九个人死了，一个人活下来　　b. 死了很多次

　　c. 经历了极大的危险而活下来

_____ 2. 有了这些忠实的歌迷的支持，他的事业才会更加 如日中天 。

　　a. 刚刚起步　　b. 事业兴盛　　c. 开始下滑

_____ 3. 侵略者常常为自己发动战争的强盗行径 涂脂抹粉 。

　　a. 对丑事进行美化　　b. 在书上乱涂乱画　　c. 化妆

_____ 4. 在中国的封建社会，皇权是 至高无上 的。

　　a. 什么都能做　　b. 地位最高的　　c. 并不是最高的

五、选词填空

◆ Choose the most appropriate word and fill in the blanks

| 如此 | 就 | 以便 | 据 |
| 即使 | 以……为…… | 尤其 | |

1. _____估计，欧洲每年要花7000多万欧元用于发展农业科学技术。

2. 两国总理_____如何促进经济发展和相互合作达成很多共识。

3. 因为这次地震发生在山区，救援队派出了三架直升机，_____及时救出受伤的灾民。

4. _____在寒冷的冬天，我们也要坚持锻炼。

5. 虽然只是一个普通职员，他却对公司的大小事务十分关心，节假日也常到公司加班。大家都称赞他_____公司_____家。

6. 李老师非常喜欢运动，_____喜欢长跑。

7. 我没有想到北京的雾霾竟然_____严重！再不采取措施改善的话，后果将不堪设想。

六、句段分析

◆ Sentence analysis

1. 找出下列句子的主语、谓语和宾语(Please indicate the subject, predicate, and object in the following sentences)

(1) 布莱恩的行动破坏了数百万美国人给予NBC新闻频道的信任。

主语：_____   谓语：_____   宾语：_____

(2) 这个事件引起了美国各大媒体对新闻界的职业道德和诚信的热烈讨论。

主语：_____   谓语：_____   宾语：_____

2. 把下列句子翻译成英文(Translate the following sentences into English)

(1) 该事件不仅使威廉姆斯的可信度受到了质疑,也使人们对NBC新闻频道的操守和审查提出了批评。

(2) 这一"说谎门"事件带来的最重要启示是,身居高位的人即使有了至高无上的地位和荣誉,仍然可能通过造假提高自己的声誉,以便让人更加仰慕、崇拜他。

七、小作文

◆ Short essay

你怎么看新闻报道不真实的问题？请分析一下有哪些原因使新闻记者报道虚假新闻。

（200-300字，请在你的作文中尽量用上本课所学的生词和句型结构。200-300 characters; please do your best to use the words and grammar patterns learned in this lesson.）

第8课 外媒热议：中国开放"二胎"政策

一、请用英文解释下列词的意思
Please give the meanings of the following words in English

研究 _____   政界 _____

美媒 _____   涨价 _____

历史学家 _____   出口率 _____

减少 _____   供养 _____

二、完成构词
Complete the following word constructions

兴奋剂	_____剂	_____剂	_____剂
注射器	_____器	_____器	_____器
药物	_____物	_____物	_____物
奖牌	_____牌	_____牌	_____牌
选手	_____手	_____手	_____手
文坛	_____坛	_____坛	_____坛
畸形	_____形	_____形	_____形
直升机	_____机	_____机	_____机

41

三、区分下面词汇的用法并完成填空

♦ *Please note the different usages of the following words and fill in the blanks*

1. 损害、害

（损害 is usually used in a more abstract sense and is a written/formal expression while 害 is often used in a more concrete sense and is a spoken/informal expression.）

① _____别人的利益；_____自己；_____名誉

② _____相互间的信任；_____朋友；_____夫妻关系

2. 解读、读

（解读 is usually used in a more abstract sense and is a written/formal expression while 读 is often used in a more concrete sense and is a spoken/informal expression.）

① _____生育政策；_____书；_____信；

② _____报；_____政府的新规定；_____电子邮件；_____新闻

3. 规避、避

（规避 is usually used in a more abstract sense and is a written/formal expression while 避 is often used in a more concrete sense and is a spoken/informal expression.）

① _____风险；_____风；_____雨；

② _____危险；_____税；_____法律惩罚

4. 竞争、争

（竞争 is usually used in a more abstract sense and is a written/formal expression while 争 is often used in a more concrete sense and is a spoken/informal expression.）

① 现在的职场_____很激烈。

② 你怎么什么都跟他_____呢？

| Lesson 8
外媒热议:中国开放"二胎"政策

③ 美国和中国在国际地位上存在着_____。

④ 你家的经济条件这么好,就不要跟别的学生_____奖学金了。

四、找出与阴影词语最接近的解释

♦ Choose the expression that is closest in meaning to the shaded word or phrase

_____ 1. 美国民众对奥巴马的医疗保险政策 褒贬不一。

a. 评价不一致　　b. 有相同的看法　　c. 都很赞赏

_____ 2. 美国民主党和共和党在这个问题上的看法 大同小异。

a. 完全一样　　b. 完全不同　　c. 没有很大的不同

_____ 3. 在社会老龄化方面,中国可以和日本 相提并论。

a. 没有相同的地方　　b. 没有可比性　　c. 有可比性

_____ 4. 事物都不是 一成不变 的。

a. 完全不变　　b. 完全改变了　　c. 改变了一些

_____ 5. 他这么做是为了得到别人的好感,这是 显而易见 的。

a. 很容易看出　　b. 不容易看出　　c. 很难看出

_____ 6. 这两年北京和上海的房价 水涨船高!

a. 受全国影响而涨价　　b. 受全国影响而降价

c. 不受全国影响而涨价

五、选词填空

♦ Choose the most appropriate word and fill in the blanks

| 自从 | 一直 | 该 | 通过 | 一旦 |
| 导致 | 所 | 一向 | 随着 | |

1. _____电脑信息化的发展，人们的联络方式越来越快捷方便。

2. _____上个世纪八十年代以来，中国实行了改革开放的政策。

3. 《参考消息》十分关注美国大选，_____报时常转载美联社的消息。

4. 他_____提出的问题代表了一部分人的看法。

5. _____讨论，我们大家取得了一致意见。

6. _____发生紧急情况，就打911。

7. "一个中国"是美国政府的_____主张。

8. 近十年来上海的房价_____上升。

9. 最近北京的物价又上涨了10%，是什么原因_____这次的物价上涨呢？

六、句段分析

◆ Sentence analysis

1. 找出下列句子的主语、谓语和宾语 (Please indicate the subject, predicate, and object in the following sentences)

(1) 2013年11月15日，中国政府决定启动实施一方是独生子女的夫妇可生育两个孩子的政策。

主语：_____ 谓语：_____ 宾语：_____

(2) 计划生育政策自从1980年开始实施以来一直受到官方的称赞。

主语：_____ 谓语：_____ 宾语：_____

2. 把下列句子翻译成英文 (Translate the following sentences into English)

(1) 一直关注中国计划生育政策的英国人口老龄化学会学者皮尔·波特认为，近40年的计划生育政策可以说是中国人口战略史上的成功一步。

(2) 北京、上海等城市数以千万计的老龄群体越来越依赖国家的养老金生活，这让政府的公共项目开支不得不进一步缩减，让社会公共福利质量出现下降。

七、小作文

◆ Short essay

根据你的理解，中国的"二胎"政策跟1979年以来推行的计划生育政策有什么不同？在你看来，中国政府为什么要实行"二胎"的政策？中国的人口控制政策对世界的人口发展和经济平衡有什么样的影响？

（200-300字，请在你的作文中尽量用上本课所学的生词和句型结构。200-300 characters; please do your best to use the words and grammar patterns learned in this lesson.）